A YEAR IN THE SECRET GARDEN

VALARIE BUDAYR & MARILYN SCOTT-WATERS

Wishing You Many Wonderful Adventures in the Secret Garden.

Best Wishes

Valarie Budayr

A Year in the Secret Garden

Text and photo Copyright 2014
Illustration Copyright 2014

All rights reserved. No part of this book may be reproduced, transmitted, or stored in an information retrieval system in any form or by any means, graphic, electronic, or mechanical, including photocopying, taping, and recording, without prior written permission from the publisher.

Editor: K. Adventure Boggs
Graphic Design: K. Adventure Boggs
Book Cover : Marilyn Scott-Waters

First edition 2014

Library of Congress Control Number: 2014916969

e-ISBN: 978-1-936426-16-4

p-ISBN: 978-1-936426-17-1

This book was typeset in

Adobe Caslon Pro,
Apollo ASM, and
ALWAYSHERETOO.

Audrey Press
P.O. Box 6113
Maryville, TN 37802

Visit us at www.audreypress.com

Printed in the USA
Signature Book Printing, www.sbpbooks.com

VB: *I lovingly dedicate this book to my three children, Zaina, Miriam, and Omar, with whom I've had many adventures. Much love to all of you.*

MSW: *To my awesome mom, Joan, and my amazing mother-in-law, Margaret, wonderful mothers who love gardens, birds, and life in general.*

Acknowledgments

Valarie Budayr

I'd like to thank all of the incredible talent who worked and contributed to this book: Marilyn Scott-Waters, Kitten Adventure Boggs, Becky Flansburg, and Hannah Rials, as well as the whole Audrey Press team: Terry Green, Caley Walsh, Theresa Scholes, and Lara Niedberding.

A huge thank you to my family who continue to love, support, and inspire me on a daily basis.

To my coffee, mommy, and travel friends which make life a true adventure.

To my constant and loyal cat companions, Oskar and Marcel. My writing table wouldn't be the same without you.

To all of our fantastic readers near and far!!! Thank you for all your support. We create thinking of you the entire way.

Marilyn Scott-Waters

I'd like to thank my friends Marcia Popp, Bob Singer and Alice Provensen for their kind words of artistic advice and encouragement. And thanks to the Mencats, I love you so much, but not so much to McQueen, who slept on my keyboard, knocked over ink bottles with his tail and pretty much was a general nuisance.

CONTENTS

September

Indian Style Chicken Curry 13
Rangoli 15
Magic Carpets. 17
Misselthwaite Manor 18
Character Study: Mary Lennox 19
Ploughman's Lunch 21

October

Cutouts of
Secret Garden Characters 22
Planting Bulbs 23
The English Garden 25
Character Study: Mrs Medlock 26

November

Hot Oatcakes 28
Jump Rope. 30
A Plastic Bag Jump Rope 30
Jump Rope Rhymes 32
Shovel, Shovel, Spade 34
Character Study: Ben Weatherstaff 35

MORE CONTENTS

December

Bringing in the Evergreen 37
Yorkshire Pudding Toad-in-a-Hole 37
The Oak King vs.
The Holly King 41
The Story of Mistletoe 42
Character Study: Martha Sowerby 43

January

Parkin Cake 44
Wutherin' Wind Flags 46
Ice Disks 47
Yorkshire Phrasebook 49
Character Study : Dickon Sowerby 53
Perfectly Good Porridge
with Treacle 55

February

Oaten Pipe 56
Garden in a Jar 59
Death in Victorian England 60
Character Study: Archibald Craven 62
Sticky Toffee Pudding 63

FURTHER CONTENTS

March

Nest Building 65
Seed Paper & Packets. 67
Grow-Me Seed Paper 67
Seed Packets. 69
Class of Hunger. 70
Character Study : Colin Craven 71

April

Robin Cake 74
Dickon's Felt Creatures. 78
The World of Mason Bees 81
Making a Mason Bee House 81
British Money. 83
Old British Money 83
Character Study: Dr. Craven 85

May

Freezer Strawberry Jam. 87
Planting a Rose Bush 88
Wheelbarrow Race 89
Wheelbarrow 90
Spot-Sitting. 91
Character Study: Lilias Craven 92
A Midsummer Garden Tea Party. 93

CONTENTS, CONTINUED

June

Ladybug Sandwiches 94
Rainbow Fruit Kabobs 95
Simply Divine
Lemon Cookies 96
Daisy Chain Crowns 97
Midsummer Dancing Ribbon Wreaths 98
Flower Pressing 98
Character Study:
Victorian/Edwardian Family Life 100
The Secret Meal. 102

July

Tin Foil Breakfast. 103
The Cooking Campfire 104
Creating a Garden Journal 107
Colin's Exercises 108
Blindfolded Garden Walk 109
Colin's Magic Chant and Affirmations 111
Rock and Stone Search 113
Character Study: Susan Sowerby. 119
Scones and Ginger Tea 120

August

A Taste of Summer 121
Paper Garden Model 123
Garden Games for Family and Friends 127

CONTENTS, CONCLUDED

Blind Man's Bluff 127
Red Rover 127
Character Study:
Frances Hodgson Burnett 128

Resources 131

Meet the Author 138

Other Books and Adventures
by Valarie Budayr 139

Meet the Illustrator & Toymaker 140

Other Books and Adventures
by Marilyn Scott-Waters 141

Audrey Press Credits 142

PREFACE

Many moments of our childhoods were spent inside the pages of *The Secret Garden*, wandering through the mysterious hallways of Misselthwaite Manor, and sharing the adventures of Mary, Colin, and Dickon. We dreamed of finding the lost key ourselves and to be able to visit the magical garden and watch it bloom into life.

The book you hold in your hands is a guidebook from the imaginings of two little girls who grew up and decided that they had found the key to the Secret Garden after all and could explore it anytime they wanted.

Month by month, you too can experience a year in the garden, with activities, crafts, and games, a mixture of character stories, easy-to-make paper toys, as well as delicious recipes from the kitchen of Misselthwaite Manor. We have created *A Year in the Secret Garden* to be the key to unlocking this beloved childhood tale for you and your family to enjoy and experience together. It is our wish to encourage curiosity, exploration, creativity, and discovery.

Wishing you many happy moments inside your very own Secret Garden.

Happy Reading!
Valarie and Marilyn

A YEAR IN THE SECRET GARDEN

VALARIE BUDAYR & MARILYN SCOTT-WATERS

September

> *"I believe, of course, in magic. Magic is the bringing about of unbelievable things through an obstinate faith that nothing is too good to be true…"*
>
> —Frances Burnett Hodges

The Secret Garden is first and foremost a story about magic and bringing things to life. A hidden garden is set to be discovered and tended, returned to its beauty and former glory. Like the garden, two children who have been tended but not nurtured are getting set to blossom and grow as the mysteries and secrets of nature make themselves known.

This journey begins far away from the heath and moors of Yorkshire in the stifling heat of India, where Mary Lennox lives with her parents, but is mostly cared for by an Aya who tells her stories about Rajas, elephants and tigers, and of course, magic.

India is a country filled with diverse people, languages, and cultures. A common smell and taste among them is curry, a flavor Mary Lennox was familiar with. The dish below is common in Yorkshire England. Many thousands of British served in India with the British military. When they returned to England, they brought some of the flavors and cuisine back with them.

Indian Style Chicken Curry

Serves 4.

INGREDIENTS:

- 3 green finger chilies, roughly chopped (optional – they're spicy!)
- ½ tsp turmeric
- ½ tsp curry
- ½ tsp ground coriander
- ¼ tsp ground cinnamon
- 2 tsp ginger root, peeled and finely grated
- 4 garlic cloves, roughly chopped
- ½ tsp salt
- 10 shallots, topped, and cut in half
- 4 tbsp sunflower or groundnut oil
- 2–4 cloves
- 1 lb boneless and skinless chicken breasts, cut into 4 cm pieces
- 1 8 oz can coconut milk
- Plain basmati rice to serve

[INDIAN STYLE CHICKEN CURRY, CONTINUED]

In a blender or with a pestle and mortar, blend the chilies, curry, turmeric, coriander, cinnamon, ginger, garlic, salt and two shallots with 1 tbsp of the oil and 2 tbsp cold water to make a coarse to medium paste.

In a large bowl, combine the chicken and the spice paste so all the chicken pieces are coated; allow to marinate for 20 minutes, or longer if possible.

Heat the remaining oil in a heavy-based frying pan or whatever you use to make pancakes. Add the cloves and fry for a minute. Then add the chicken and fry for 5 minutes until the spices become fragrant (leave the remaining paste in the bowl for later).

Tip in the remaining shallots and continue frying for 10–12 minutes until they are lightly brown on the outside.

Pour 1/2 cup cold water and the coconut milk in the bowl with the remaining spice paste and combine. Pour over the chicken and mix well.

Simmer for 5-7 minutes until the chicken is cooked.

Serve hot with plain basmati rice.

Rangoli

Rangoli is a type of decorative design made in living rooms and courtyards during Hindu festivals. The designs are made using bright colors, and are usually drawn by women. They are intended as sacred areas to welcome Hindu deities, and contain ancient symbols passed down from one generation to another. Thought to bring good luck, rangoli designs reflect the traditions, folklore, and practices of each particular region of India.

Rangoli designs are made of colored rice, dry flour, colored sand and flower petals, and can be simple geometric shapes, a lotus flower, deities, or more elaborate designs. There are both wet and dry methods for creating them.

Paving Stone Rangoli

Supplies:

- **Paving Stone**
- **Chalk**
- **Food coloring**
- **White flour**
- **Long ruler**
- **Thick paintbrush**

(Warning: The reason for using a paving stone is that rangoli can stain a driveway or sidewalk permanently.)

[RANGOLI, CONTINUED]

Use your ruler to draw out a grid of dots. For more intricate designs place your dots closer together – for simple designs, further apart. A good starting point for your first rangoli is a tile 18 inches by 18 inches, with your dots 1 inch apart.

Now draw your design on the grid with the chalk (perhaps sketching it out first on grid paper).

Mix together half a cup of flour, a few drops of food coloring, and a little water until it forms a paste about the texture of Elmer's glue. Repeat for each color you are using. Using your flour pastes, paint the colors into your design.

If you're working with young children, draw out the design first and let them color it in.

An alternative is to fill the design in with colored sand instead of wet flour.

Magic Carpets

Just like in the stories Mary's Aya told her in India, a magic carpet can take you anywhere you want to go. After the tragedy of her parents death, Mary was sent to her uncle's house, Misselthwaite Manor, with instructions to "keep out of trouble" and, more importantly, to "stay out of the way." Left to her own devices, Mary began to explore the gardens and discover what lay within its hedges and garden beds. Perhaps she collected those things and took them back to her bedroom to keep them safe, or maybe she created magic carpets with her newly found treasures to take her to lands and worlds unknown.

How to Make a Magic Carpet

Go out into the garden and collect stones, sticks, leaves, branches, cones, bark, berries, seeds, and anything else nature might provide. To create a magic carpet, create an outline with the stones, sticks, or branches and fill it in with colorful leaves, berries, nuts, cones, and seeds. You can create a different sort of magic carpet each season as nature changes. Creating magic carpets is a perfect way to collect treasures and capture the experience of the place and moment you're gathering in.

Misselthwaite Manor

Built over 600 years ago and seated at the edge of a Moor, Misselthwaite Manor appears lonely and gloomy from a distance. From its very name, after a small brown bird known as a Missel thrush and a thwaite – a "bit of land," Misselthwaite Manor begins to share the secrets of the story to come. Its walls contain over 100 locked rooms holding long forgotten secrets. The entrance is a massive oak door studded with big iron nails and bound by large iron bars. It opens into an enormous, dimly lit entrance hall.

The painted portraits hanging on the walls and suits of armor standing in the foyer did not give Mary a welcoming feeling, but one of gloom. On her way to Misselthwaite Manor, she learned from Mrs. Medlock of her uncle, Lord Craven, who was widowed, a hunchback, and living in this ancient old house. For Mary, it was something like living in a fairytale.

Among the secrets of the 100 locked rooms, of her parents, and of her aunt, Mary is quietly hidden away in a distant room among the wandering corridors of Misselthwaite Manor. Lord Craven does not want to be reminded of what he doesn't want to see.

Soon, though, the gardens surrounding Misselthwaite Manor unfold their secrets and healing upon the children and adults who live there. The 100 rooms, the hidden garden gate – all are unlocked to heal the past and create the future.

Character Study: Mary Lennox

Mary Lennox is a lonely little girl who, though she lived with her parents in India, was left to be raised by servants.

She is described as ugly, ill-tempered, and viciously demanding, but this is not to be blamed on poor Mary. Her mother, who was quite beautiful, was disappointed in her daughter's ugliness and state of constant sickliness. She refused to see Mary.

Mistress Mary never wished for friends. She disliked people older than her and younger than her, but worst of all were people her own age. Mary did not need anyone.

Mary's only pleasure at this point was playing gardening – her only comfort was to sit under a tree and play with flowers which she would make into "mounds of sound."

Shortly after her parents' deaths from cholera, Mary was sent to live with the parson, where the garden remained her place of solace – she played the same sort of games there.

[Mary Lennox, continued]

Upon arriving in England, Mary continues to be quite contrary, rude, standoffish, and sullen, but with the nudging and encouragement of the young upstairs maid, Martha, Mary goes out into the garden where she meets Ben Weatherstaff. There she becomes intensely interested in what is going on around her. The loneliness she once felt is placated by the nature around her and her daily discoveries. For the first time in her life, Mary has real affection for other people. Her maidservant Martha Sowerby becomes a sisterly friend to her. Martha's brother Dickon mesmerizes Mary with his magical ways with animals. Soon Mary befriends her cousin Colin, and together inside the walls of the secret garden they miraculously restore their own lives and each others, unveiling their secrets and creating hope for a promising future.

October

Ploughman's Lunch

As Mary was bundled up to go out into the garden, they often sent her with a lunch basket. As it is common throughout all of England, a ploughman's lunch is the perfect sort of meal for one out in the fields or gardens.

THE PERFECT PLOUGHMAN'S LUNCH CONSISTS OF:

Freshly baked bread
1 slice of cooked meat such as: turkey, chicken, roast beef, or ham
Chutney
1 dill pickle
Radishes
Celery
Coleslaw
Apple slices

Cutouts of Secret Garden Characters

22

Planting Bulbs

Mistress Mary, quite contrary,
How does your garden grow?
With silver bells, and cockle shells,
And marigolds all in a row.

Though Mary was taunted by this rhyme, it still holds to reason that if we want the beautiful flowers of spring, we need to prepare for them in the fall. October is a perfect time to plant bulbs in the Northern Hemisphere and April in the Southern Hemisphere. Whenever the temperature outside gets to 60 degrees Fahrenheit, you can start planting bulbs.

Bulbs grow best in a location with full sun. Choose planting beds where bulb foliage will receive at least 6 hours of sun during spring through summer. Most bulb species also prefer well-drained, not soggy, soil. Here's how to plant bulbs:

SUPPLIES

- A variety of bulbs
- Trowel or bulb-planting tool
- Shovel
- Bulb fertilizer
- Mulch
- Water and nozzle

[Planting Bulbs, continued]

1. Dig Holes

Dig individual bulb holes or one wide hole to plant groups of bulbs. Digging up the whole bed makes bulb spacing, layering, and soil amending easier. The depth of the hole should equal three to four times the bulb height. For example, dig a 6- to 8-inch-deep hole for a 2-inch-high bulb.

2. Arrange Bulbs

Set the bulbs in a planting bed or in separate planting holes with their roots or basal plate downward. Space bulbs according to supplier's recommendations. In general, smaller bulbs are planted closer together than larger bulbs. Fill the planting hole with soil and firm it gently.

3. Water and Mulch

Water the bulbs right after planting to help initiate growth. In mild-winter areas, mulch right after planting to help keep soil cool and moist. Apply mulch after soil freezes in cold-winter areas to prevent the ground from heaving during winter thaws and pushing the bulbs too close to the surface.

The English Garden

Since Roman times in England, gardens have always played an important role in the lives of the British.

Misselthwaite Manor would have a variety of gardens on the property. When Mary first went exploring, she met Ben Weatherstaff, who was working in the kitchen garden at the time. A house like Misselthwaite would have at least 3 or 4 kitchen gardens averaging in size between 1-1/2 and 5 acres each.

The kitchen gardens included an orchard which supported a large variety of fruit, vegetables, and herbs. These gardens were walled to keep out thieving town folk and wandering sheep and cattle. To increase the fruit yield, many trees were attached to the garden walls to give them more exposure to warmth and light, thereby giving them higher yields.

An estate like Misselthwaite Manor would produce all of its own food. Mrs. Loomis, the cook, would consult with the head gardener Mr. Roach, about what he should plant so there would be enough food to feed the entire household including the serving staff.

Set within the walled gardens is the secret garden, originally planted with roses along the walls and trellises. After many years of neglect, the dead wood was cleared away. The secret garden once again became a sheltered paradise of colors and perfumes – a mass spectacle of roses, gillyflowers, lavender, and scented philadelphus.

Character Study: Mrs Medlock

> "She was a stout woman, with very red cheeks and sharp black eyes. She wore a very purple dress, a black silk mantle with jet fringe on it and a black bonnet with purple velvet flowers which stuck up and trembled when she moved her head."

Mrs. Medlock was Mr. Archibald Craven's housekeeper. She held the top position among the female domestic help in the house. Most well to do families in England hired a housekeeper to manage the rest of the household staff in service to the family. All of the maids, kitchen staff, and gardeners served under the guidance of the housekeeper.

One of the most important jobs of the housekeeper was to insure the safe keeping of all the silver and other goods in the house and the food. She carried every key to the house and safe guarded that everything was locked up tight all of the time. All of the goods and food were regularly counted to make sure nothing was stolen.

The name Mrs. Medlock has double meaning as it is her name and she is the one who carries all of the keys. She is a woman to be trusted. Whether a housekeeper was married or not she was always called "Mrs."

Like the servants in India, the British servants had to obey the rules set before them by the master of the house. Mrs. Medlock is diligent, meticulous, and obedient of all Master Craven's odd rules. Underneath that stern exterior, though, Mrs. Medlock is a kind person who generally cares about people. She and Susan

Sowerby, Dickon and Martha's mother, were childhood friends. In the end, she too sees the miracle of Colin's blooming and how it was brought about by his cousin Mary.

November

Hot Oatcakes

For centuries the citizens of Great Britain have eaten oatcakes, also known as haver cakes. In Susan Sowerby's house, oatcakes were cooked on a flat iron or griddle pan over the fire. Those lucky enough to be home during oatcake frying received hot, fluffy oatcakes with butter on them. The rest were left to cool and get crispy. Oftentimes they were hung on the cottage ceiling to eat later.

Ingredients

- 1 cup milk
- 1 cup water
- 2-1/4 tsp active dry yeast and 1 tsp sugar
- 2 cups finely ground oatmeal
- 1/2 cup whole wheat flour
- 1 tsp salt
- 2 tsp canola oil for frying pan

Instructions

In a saucepan, mix the milk and water. Set to low heat until the mixture is lukewarm to the touch.

Pour the warmed mixture into a large mixing bowl. Crumble the yeast into the mixture and stir it until it is dissolved. Add the sugar and set aside for 5 minutes.

Stir the oatmeal, flour, and salt into the milk mixture.

Add water if necessary.

Cover the bowl with a damp towel or plastic wrap and set it aside in a warm place for about an hour.

Lightly grease a frying pan and place it over medium high heat.

Stir the oatcake batter. Add 1/4 cup of water and stir some more.

Spoon about 2/3 cup of the batter into the hot pan, spreading it slightly to make a thin oval pancake in the middle of the pan.

Cook the oatcake for just a few minutes, until it is set but not browned on the bottom. Turn the oatcake and cook it briefly on the other side.

Serve the oatcake hot with butter, jam, or marmalade.

You can dry the leftovers on a cooling rack and store them in a covered container. They're perfect to eat later with cheese or jam.

Jump Rope

"The skipping-rope
was a wonderful thing.
She counted and skipped, and skipped and counted,
until her cheeks were quite red,
and she was more interested than she had ever been
since she was born. The sun was shining
and a little wind was blowing – not a rough wind,
but one which came in delightful little gusts
and brought a fresh scent of newly turned earth
with it. She skipped round the fountain garden,
and up one walk and down another.
She skipped at last into the kitchen-garden and saw
Ben Weatherstaff digging and talking to his robin,
which was hopping about him.
She skipped down the walk toward him
and he lifted his head and looked at her
with a curious expression.
She had wondered if he would notice her.
She wanted him to see her skip."

A Plastic Bag Jump Rope

SUPPLIES

- **Many plastic grocery store bags**
- **Scissors**
- **Duct tape**

INSTRUCTIONS

Take a plastic bag, cutting it open on the sides and bottom to make one flat piece.

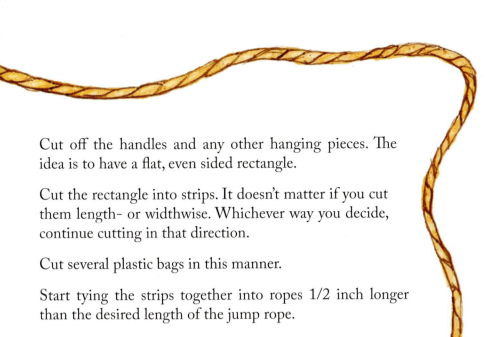

Cut off the handles and any other hanging pieces. The idea is to have a flat, even sided rectangle.

Cut the rectangle into strips. It doesn't matter if you cut them length- or widthwise. Whichever way you decide, continue cutting in that direction.

Cut several plastic bags in this manner.

Start tying the strips together into ropes 1/2 inch longer than the desired length of the jump rope.

Jump rope lengths are as follows:

> 10 yrs and under: 8 feet
> 10 yrs and over : 9 feet.

Make 12 long plastic bag strips at the desired length.

Take 6 plastic bag strip ropes and anchor them to a table with duct tape.

Using 2 strips for each braid course, braid the strips to the end to make a long braided jump rope. Tie it off on the end with duct tape.

Braid the next 12 strips like the previous one, sealing each off with duct tape.

Take the taped off ends of the braided jump ropes and anchor them to a table with duct tape.

Tightly twist the two braids together.

Wrap duct tape around each end of the jump rope to make the handles.

Jump Rope Rhymes

"Mary skipped round all the gardens and round the orchard, resting every few minutes. At length she went to her own special walk and made up her mind to try if she could skip the whole length of it. It was a good long skip and she began slowly, but before she had gone half-way down the path she was so hot and breathless that she was obliged to stop. She did not mind much, because she had already counted up to thirty."

COLUMBUS WENT TO SEA

Columbus went to sea, sea, sea.
To see what he could see, see, see.
But all that he could see, see, see
Was the bottom on the sea, sea, sea.

CINDERELLA DRESSED IN GREEN

Cinderella, dressed in green,
Went upstairs to eat ice cream.
How many spoonfuls did she eat?
One, two, three, ...

Mary Mack

Mary Mack, dressed in black
Silver buttons down her back.
Asked her Ma for fifteen cents
To see the elephant jump the fence.

He jumped so high
He touched the sky
And won't come back
Until the fourth of July.

Not Last Night

Not last night
But the night before
Twenty four robbers
Knocking at my door.
As I ran out,
They ran in.
I hit them over the head
With a rolling pin.

The King of France

The King of France
Wet his pants
Right in the middle
Of a wedding dance.
How many puddles
Did he make?
One, two, three, ...

Shovel, Shovel, Spade

Daily, Ben Weatherstaff works patiently in his garden. Each season brings new delights and challenges while Ben works diligently. When Mary Lennox first discovers the vast gardens at Misselthwaite Manor, she tries her best to befriend old Ben. After many years of working alone, he doesn't need the company of a little girl who constantly asks questions.

Mary goes in search for her own "piece of earth"; once she finds it, she sends a note and some money to Dickon to ask him to buy her garden tools and seeds so she can dig and plant.

RULES

Shovel, Shovel, Spade is a take off of the famous children's game Duck, Duck, Goose.

You will need at least 4–5 players.

All the players except the person who is It sit in a circle. It walks around the circle tapping each player on the head, saying "shovel" each time until he/she decides to tap someone and say "spade." That person becomes the spade and runs after It, trying to tag him or her before It can take his/her seat. If It successfully reaches and sits in the spade's seat without being tagged, the spade becomes the new It. If the spade tags It, the spade keeps his/her spot in the circle and It continues to be It for another turn.

Character Study: Ben Weatherstaff

On one of her first explorations into the gardens of Misselthwaite Manor, Mary encounters Ben Weatherstaff, an old grumpy gardener. Upon their first meeting, he introduces Mary to the red breasted Robin that lives in the garden. The robin along with Ben and Mary are grieving the loss of someone. The robin is sad because it's been left behind by its family. Ben is doubly sad at the death of his wife and the loss of his boss Mistress Craven, Colin's mother.

Ben Weatherstaff was kept on at Misselthwaite because he was Mistress Craven's favorite gardener. Upon her death, however, he – like everyone else – was locked out of the Secret Garden. Out of devotion to Mistress Craven he tended her locked garden by climbing over the wall with a ladder.

Though he is rough around the edges, he is a loyal and kind friend who unveils the secrets of the garden to Mary, opening up a new, magical world to discover.

December

In December, night falls over the world. Sunrise comes later and the day darkens earlier. The land, which was rich in life just a few short weeks ago, slumbers in a veil of gray mist that is only lightened by snow.

Pine and spruce trees, rosemary, winter berry, laurel, holly, and mistletoe are known as evergreens. They conquer the darkness of winter with their green leaves and branches, white or red berries, and beautiful scents.

The evergreen tree symbolizes the light of the sun, which is undying even when it seems to have completely disappeared.

Bringing in the Evergreen

Though decorated trees have been used to celebrate winter holidays for many centuries, the Christmas tree became popular during the reign of Queen Victoria. She was married to her German cousin, Prince Albert of Germany, who brought the German custom of the Christmas tree with him to England – it was celebrated at Windsor Palace. Albert wrote, "I must now seek in the children an echo of what Ernest [his brother] and I were in the old time, of what we felt and thought; and their delight in the Christmas trees is not less than ours used to be."

The Victorian Christmas, into the Edwardian era, attempted to bring elements of the countryside into the house during the holiday season. The English not only placed Christmas trees in their homes, but also a great supply of evergreen wreaths decorated with ribbon, dried apples, and berries.

Yorkshire Pudding Toad-in-a-Hole

No one really knows where the name of this dish comes from. Perhaps it's that toads hide during the day in damp places. They like to burrow into soft ground, to which they return day after day. They sit inside the entrance of their burrow and pounce on any passing insect. This Toad-in-a-Hole recipe turns an easy Yorkshire pudding recipe into a filling meal by adding sausages to it. One could say that these sausages sitting in the Yorkshire pudding batter resemble toads in a hole.

This makes a nice and easy dinner, and is also tasty with fresh vegetables and onion gravy.

[Yorkshire Pudding Toad-in-a-Hole, continued]

Ingredients

- 1½ cups all purpose flour
- 1 tsp salt
- Pinch of black pepper
- 3 eggs beaten
- 1½ cups milk
- 2 tbsp melted butter
- 1 tbsp vegetable oil
- 1 lb pork or beef sausages

Instructions

In a large bowl, whisk together the flour with the salt and a pinch of pepper. Make a well in the center of the flour. Pour the eggs, milk, and melted butter into the well and whisk into the flour until smooth. Cover and let stand for 30 minutes.

Coat the bottom and sides of an 8×12 or a 9×9 casserole dish with vegetable oil. Place a rack in the bottom third of the oven. Put the empty dish on the rack. Preheat the oven with the dish in it to 425°F (220°C).

While the oven is coming to temperature, heat a tablespoon of vegetable oil in a skillet on medium high. Add the sausages and brown them on at least a couple of sides.

When the sausages have browned and the dish in the oven is hot, pull the oven rack out a bit, put the sausages in the casserole dish, and pour the batter over the sausages. Cook for about 25 minutes or until the batter has risen and is golden brown.

Serve at once. **Yields 4–6 servings.**

Winter Bird Feeders

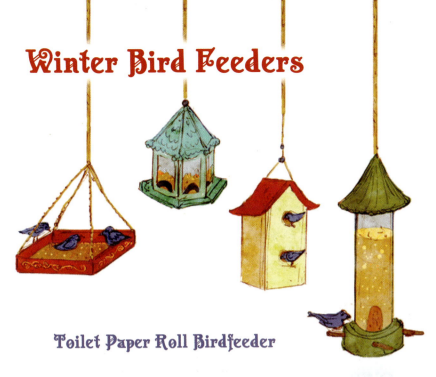

Toilet Paper Roll Birdfeeder

SUPPLIES

- **Empty toilet paper roll**
- **Organic peanut butter**
- **Table knife**
- **Birdseed**
- **String or yarn**
- **Scissors**

INSTRUCTIONS

Spread peanut butter around the entire toilet paper roll with the table knife.

Put the seed in a shallow pan or tin pie pan.

Roll the toilet paper roll in the birdseed.

[WINTER BIRD FEEDERS, CONTINUED]

Cut a length of string or yarn long enough to go through the paper roll tube plus some overhang.

Place the string/yarn through the tube and tie a knot.

Hang the feeder outside on a tree. Or, instead of attaching string/yarn, just slide the toilet paper roll over a branch.

Teacup Bird Feeder

SUPPLIES

- **Teacup and saucer**
- **E6000 glue**
- **Birdseed**
- **String**
- **Shepherd's hook**

INSTRUCTIONS

Glue the cup laying on its side to the saucer. Let it sit and dry overnight.

Cut two lengths of string the same size.

Loop the string through the tea cup handle, matching up the ends, and knot evenly.

Add birdseed to the saucer and inner edge of the tea cup.

Hang on a shepherd's hook outside near a tree, fountain, or in a garden bed.

The Oak King vs. The Holly King

Long ago, the land was ruled by two Kings who were twins. The younger brother wore oak leaves as a crown, and was known as the Oak King. The older brother wore holly leaves as a crown, and was known as the Holly King.

Each brother felt he knew the best way to rule the land; they quarreled over it constantly. The Oak King wanted the land to be bright, hot, and sunny for the entire year. The Holly King wanted the land to be dark, cold, and slumbering for the whole year.

Both Kings loved a beautiful Lady. She loved them both as well and hated to watch them fight. She told them to share the land between them – one half of the year for the Oak King, the other half of the year for the Holly King.

The brothers couldn't be persuaded to stop their fighting. One hot day when the sun was high in the sky and it seemed night would never come, the Holly King drew his sword against his brother, and they fought. Although the Oak King fought bravely, the Holly King struck a mortal blow, and the Oak King fell.

"My brother!" cried the Holly King, holding the bleeding body of the Oak King in his arms. As the Oak King cried, the Lady bundled up the body of the Oak King, told the Holly King that he must rule the land, and took the Oak King away.

[THE OAK KING VS. THE HOLLY KING, CONTINUED]

Each day, the hours of daylight grew shorter. Each night, the moon rode in the sky for a bit longer. The days grew shorter and cooler, the nights, longer and colder. Snow started falling and blowing. The Holly King could think of nothing but his brother.

Finally, the land was bare and dead, and all plants slept under the cloak of snow. Many animals slept through the cold times, and those that didn't had a hard time finding food and shelter. One night, when it seemed like the sun would never rise again, the Lady came to the Holly King and said, "Don't despair, your brother isn't dead. Here he is to take his turn at ruling."

There stood the Oak King, young again and healthy, and the Holly King happily stepped aside for his brother to take his place as King of the land.

The days grew longer and warmer. The moon rode in the sky for less and less time. The land grew green again, and the plants and animals awoke. Each year the cycle continued, one brother ruling the green time, the other the dark time.

The Story of Mistletoe

Mistletoe is still hung up in farmhouses and kitchens at Christmas, and young men have the privilege of kissing girls under it, plucking each time a berry from the bush. When the berries are all plucked, the privilege ceases.

Character Study: Martha Sowerby

"She was a round, rosy, good-natured looking creature…"

Martha is Mary's kind, sweet-tempered maidservant and another important element of Mary's change in personality and lifestyle. Mrs. Medlock gave Martha – only a common daughter of the moor – work at Misselthwaite Manor out of kindness to her mother, Susan Sowerby. Not coached in the proper manner of an estate maidservant, Martha often slips back into her Yorkshire dialect and is very frank and outspoken, often commenting on Mary's inability to look after herself.

It is Martha who tells Mary about Mrs. Craven's walled garden, which has been closed and locked since her death.

January

Parkin Cake

Yorkshire parkin cake is the northern English version of gingerbread, and is unique because it incorporates oats. It is eaten throughout the winter, but is a staple on Bonfire Night, which celebrates a famous Yorkshireman named Guy Fawkes. Fawkes is noted for trying to blow up the British House of Parliament in 1605. Every November 5th, Britain has a great fireworks display, eating parkin cake as they watch.

Ingredients

- **8 oz soft butter**
- **½ cup soft, dark brown sugar**
- **¼ cup molasses**
- **1 cup corn syrup**
- **¾ cup oatmeal**
- **1 cup self-raising flour**
- **1 tsp baking powder**
- **4 tsp ground ginger**
- **2 tsp nutmeg**
- **1 tsp pumpkin spice mix**
- **2 large eggs, beaten**
- **2 tbsp milk**

Instructions

Heat the oven to 275°F.

Grease an 8" × 8" square baking pan.

In a large heavy saucepan, melt together the butter, sugar, molasses, and corn syrup over gentle heat. Do not allow the mixture to boil – you simply need to melt these together.

In a large, spacious baking bowl stir together all the dry ingredients. Gradually add the melted butter mixture, stirring to coat all the dry ingredients, and mix thoroughly.

Gradually beat in the eggs a few tablespoons at a time.

Add the milk and stir well.

Pour the mixture into the prepared pan and cook for 1½ hours until firm, set, and a dark golden brown.

Remove the parkin from the oven and leave to cool in the pan. Once cool, store in an airtight container for a minimum of three days if you can resist eating it. The longer you let it sit, the better it tastes. Some even let it sit a week before eating it. As long as the parkin is in an airtight container, it can keep up to two weeks.

Wutherin' Wind Flags

"Martha tucked her feet under her and made herself quite comfortable.

'Listen to th' wind wutherin' round the house,' she said. 'You could bare stand up on the moor if you was out on it tonight.'

Mary did not know what 'wutherin'' meant until she listened, and then she understood. It must mean that hollow shuddering sort of roar which rushed round and round the house as if the giant no one could see were buffeting it and beating at the walls and windows to try to break in."

—From *The Secret Garden*, Chapter 5

Listen to the wutherin' wind by making flags to catch its sound and see how hard the wind is truly blowing.

SUPPLIES

- **Long pieces of brightly colored thin cotton fabric**
- **Stapler or hot glue gun**
- **Strong 3-foot stick or a piece of dowel**

INSTRUCTIONS

Choose a piece of cotton fabric and cut a long triangle 8 × 17 inches or 11 × 20 inches. The longer the tail of the flag, the more the wind will be able to move it so you can see and hear the effect.

Decorate with pieces of fabric or make designs using bleach pen.

Attach the flag to the stick using a stapler or a hot glue gun. Only an adult should do this.

On a windy day, go outside to a large open space or on a hillside. Stand still to see what the wind looks and sounds like. Next, run with your flag waving behind you – is it wutherin'?

Ice Disks

You can have a marvelous time exploring the coldness and chill of winter. Try catching the light with a lovely ice disk.

SUPPLIES

- **Tin pie pan**
- **Biscuit cutters and jam jar lids**
- **Gathered nature items**
- **String**
- **Scissors**
- **Water**

INSTRUCTIONS FOR LARGE ICE DISKS

(Do this near where you're going to freeze it – it's hard to move later on.)

1. For a large ice disk, arrange your nature items in the bottom of the pan.
2. Cut two lengths of string and place at the top center of your disk.

[ICE DISKS, CONTINUED]

3. Gently and slowly add 1/2 to 3/4 inch of water. Make any adjustments necessary to the string and nature items. They should be submerged in the water.

4. Let it set outside until frozen. If it isn't cold outside, you can use your freezer as well.

5. Once the container is frozen, release the ice disk from the pie tin. You may have to use a little bit of warm water – just enough to release it.

6. Hang from a tree with a branch supporting it underneath.

INSTRUCTIONS FOR SMALL ICE DISKS

1. Place the biscuit cutters and jam jar lids facing up on the tray.

2. Arrange your nature items inside the biscuit cutters and jam jar lids.

3. Lay a long piece of string from the middle of the container and lay the remainder over the outside edge.

4. Add water to the containers, making sure all the nature items and string are fully submerged in water.

5. If the temperature outside is freezing, place the tray outside in a place where it can freeze undisturbed. Otherwise, place the tray in the freezer.

6. Once the containers are frozen, release the ice disks from their molds. You may have to use a little warm water for this.

7. Using the string, tie your disks onto tree branches just outside a window and enjoy your icy art for as long as the freezing temperatures last.

Yorkshire Phrasebook

Can you understand the following phrases from *The Secret Garden*?

"I see tha's got back. An 'tha's browt th' young'un with thee."

"Aye that's her. How's thy missus?"

"Well enow. Th' carriage is waitin outside for thee."

"That's the moor. Does tha' like it? That's because tha'rt not used to it. Tha' thinks it's too big an bare now. But tha' will like it."

Martha, Dickon, Ben Weatherstaff, Mrs. Medlock and all of the other locals speak an English dialect called Yorkshire. It can be amusing to spice up your conversations by adding a little Yorkshire. Following is a little glossary and phrase dictionary to help you out:

YORKSHIRE WORDS

A
allus always
aye yes

B
backend Autumn
badly not in a good state of health, i.e.'How's Martha?', 'She's badly.'
bairn child
bait/bait box snack/ packed lunch
beefin(g), blubberin(g) crying
bog toilet (also, lavvy)
bonce head
bonny pretty
brant steep e.g. "tis a brant hill"
bray/braying beating e.g. "you'll get a good braying" or "I'll bray you"
butty sandwich

C

chelpin' talking
chuckin(g) your guts up being sick
chuffed pleased, excited
clarty dirty, muddy, sticky

D

dowly dull, gloomy, misty
drinkings mid-morning snack farm workers took to work
dursn't daren't

E

eeh by gum oh my God

F

faffing messing about
fair t' middlin fair, in the middle
fell moor
fettle tidy/mend
flayed, flaysome scared, scary
flippin' 'eck (flipping heck) exclamation of shock and surprise
flummoxed confused
frozzed having very cold face or fingers

G

Gaffer the boss
garth yard
giz, gizza, gizzyer give, give us, give your
gormless stupid
guff fart

I

in a bit bye
in't in the

J

jammy very lucky
jiggered very tired

K

kegs trousers/underwear

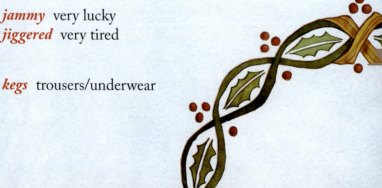

L

lake, laikin(g), larking play, playing (e.g. "Is your Lesley coming out to lake?")
leg throw
lug, lug'ole ear

M

middlin(g) ok, average
minging horrible, unpleasant
mithered, mitherin(g) irritated with something, as in "stop mitherin' me" is "stop bothering/irritating me".
(have a) monk on be grumpy, have a sulky face
missen myself e.g. "I'll do it missen"

N

narky moody, sulky, bad-tempered (also stroppy, mardy)
n'arn (now then) hello
neb nose
nowt/nout nothing

O

'ow do how are you, hello
owt anything

P

pack it in stop it
parkin ginger cake made with oats
put wood in'th oyle shut the door

R

radged angry
reet right
rum'n cheeky person/bit of a character e.g. "He's a rum'n"

S

scran food
side the pots clear the table
sithee (see thee) do you see? (often used at the end of a sentence) Also, goodbye
skell (over) fall, tip (over)
spoggs sweets
sprog child
summat something
sup drink

T

ta thanks
tarra bye
thee, tha you
thissen yourself
thwaite clearing
Tyke Yorkshire person

U

un one
up-skelled upset, knocked over, spilled

W

waint won't
while until e.g. "I'm working while seven"

wick alive or lively

Y

ya, yan one
yam home
yat hot
yune oven

Yorkshire Phrases

'appy as a pig in muck very happy, content with oneself

look frinint ye look in front of you (i.e. when walking)

more brass na brains more money than sense

near as makes n'matter close enough

neither use nor ornament expression of disapproval; useless

not enough room to swing a cat very small, cramped

Scarborough warning notice that further bad behavior will result in punishment, e.g., "You better watch it – you're on a Scarborough warning, young lady."

well, I'll go to't foot of't stairs/I'll go to our house expression of amazement

Character Study : Dickon Sowerby

"A boy was sitting under a tree, with his back against it, playing on a rough wooden pipe. He was a funny-looking boy about twelve. He looked very clean and his nose turned up and his cheeks were as red as poppies, and never had Mistress Mary seen such round and such blue eyes in any boy's face."

Dickon is the high-spirited 12-year-old brother of Mary's maidservant, Martha Sowerby. Having lived on the moor all his life, Dickon has a deeply rooted connection with the land and the animals and is often referred to as an animal charmer, though he seems to have the unique ability to charm people as well. From the moment Martha mentions Dickon and his wild animals, Mary is instantly drawn to him, later describing him as "beautiful." Physically active, thoughtful, and strong, he is Colin's polar opposite. Mary often thinks of him as a magical wood-sprite, at first afraid that he is almost too good to be true and should disappear if she should turn away. His round eyes are described as being "exactly the color of the sky over the moor."

[DICKON SOWERBY, CONTINUED]

Dickon's ability to charm animals, along with his set of panpipes, likens him to Pan – the Greek God of creativity, music, flocks, landscapes, and human nature (all of which are attributes of Dickon's personality) who wandered the hills and mountains of Arcadia playing his pipes. He feels such a deep kindred spirit with the animals that he oftentimes can't separate them from himself: "Sometimes I think perhaps I'm a bird, or a fox, or a squirrel… and I don't know it."

For Mary and Colin, Dickon holds the key to unlocking the natural world. As well as their difference in language – Dickon speaks Yorkshire while Mary and Colin speak aristocratic English – they are from different classes. Mary often comments on Dickon's patched clothing, unkempt manner, and the simple food he carries with him. Dickon, along with the secret garden, is responsible for Mary's and Colin's transformations. Dickon, having no need to change, remains a constant, loyal, kind, and informative friend throughout the story.

"… and when she sat down to her breakfast she did not glance disdainfully at her porridge and push it away, but took up her spoon and began to eat it and went on eating it until her bowl was empty."

Perfectly Good Porridge with Treacle

Serves 2 generously.

INGREDIENTS

- 1 cup oat bran
- 2 cups water
- 1 generous cup berries (fresh or frozen)
- pinch of salt
- 1–2 tablespoons honey or maple syrup
- ¼ teaspoon pure vanilla extract

TOPPINGS

- Treacle
- Nuts such as sliced almonds or toasted pecans.
- Half-and-half. It's a must. You can't have great porridge without it.
- A sprinkle of brown sugar.
- Sea salt will push this completely over the edge.

[PERFECTLY GOOD PORRIDGE, CONTINUED]

INSTRUCTIONS

In a medium pot over medium-high heat bring water, salt, and half of the fruit to a boil. Add the oat bran and honey, and stir regularly until cereal is cooked. Serve hot, topped with suggested toppings.

What is Treacle?

Treacle is any uncrystallized syrup made during the refining of sugar. In England they have two types of treacle: a pale variety known as golden syrup, which is sweet and has a light thickness to it, and a dark version known as dark or black treacle. Dark treacle is thicker, stronger and a bit bitter tasting.

In the United States, the closest thing we have to treacle is molasses.

A Halloween tradition for children in Scotland and other areas of Great Britain is to try to take a bite of a scone spread with treacle hung at head height from a piece of string.

Be brave! Try a little treacle or molasses on your porridge.

Oaten Pipe

"A boy was sitting under a tree, with his back against it, playing on a rough wooden pipe."

Out in the English countryside, many children would make reed flutes out of the dried stalk of an oat plant. This was known as an oaten pipe.

Many of you may not have dried oak stalks lying around – instead, let's make a paper flute for you to play in the garden.

SUPPLIES

- **Heavy printer paper or photo paper**
- **Tape or rubber bands**
- **Scissors**

INSTRUCTIONS

Roll your piece of paper short end to short end into a tube and secure it on each end with a rubber band or tape.

Decide which end of your tube will be the top and which one will be the bottom.

To make the air hole, cut a square hole 1½ to 2 inches from the end of the tube, and as far from the seam as you can. One easy way to do this is to cut two slits, cut out the top, fold it back and then cut off the bottom.

To make the mouthpiece, separate and bend down half of the layers between the hole you just cut and the end of the tube it's closest to. Pinch the tube so it stays put.

To sound test it, place your top lip over the top of the paper, your bottom lip under the bent part of the paper inside the tube, and blow gently. It might work right away, but usually you have to play with it to get a flute pitch out of it.

[OATEN PIPE, CONTINUED]

Troubleshooting

If you can't get a flute sound out of your oaten pipe, check the following:

- Is the air hole cut cleanly? The edge further from the mouthpiece should have all the layers together.

- Have you tried pinching or creasing where the inside layers bend down?

- Is the flute too moist? Set it aside to dry and make another flute while you wait.

Finger Holes

Once your flute can sound a pitch, try adding some finger holes for different pitched sounds. We're going to place them to either side of the central line. Unlike a recorder, placing the holes in line with the air hole and the mouthpiece can ruin the air flow of your flute and you won't get any sound.

- Start with a small hole halfway along the flute, offset to the side a little. Try blowing the flute while holding your finger over the hole to hear what it sounds like. You can make the hole larger if you'd like.

- Now make a second hole closer to the mouthpiece. Remember to start small and work larger. Try it and hear how it sounds.

Please note that it's difficult to place many pitch holes in your flute and still get a sound. Start with one or two for now, and work up to more after you become a skilled paper flute maker.

To make your oaten pipe really special, feel free to decorate it any way you want.

Garden in a Jar

Using a glass jar with a lid, you can create your own indoor version of the magical world of the Secret Garden.

SUPPLIES

- **Glass jar with a lid**
- **Small stones**
- **Planting soil**
- **Activated carbon (found at any pet store)**
- **Dried moss**
- **Live growing moss**
- **Water dropper**
- **Fun little additions such as animal figures, pinecone trees, fairies, flowers, toad stools, and such.**

INSTRUCTIONS

Cover the bottom of your jar with some small stones.

Put in a 1/2 inch layer of the planting soil.

Add a 1/2 inch layer of activated carbon.

Add a 1 to 2 inch layer of dried moss.

Cover everything with living moss.

Put in 2 or 3 dropperfuls of water.

Add your fun little magical treasures and put the lid on.

The moss will create its own little ecosystem, and only needs to be watered every 2 to 3 weeks. You'll know it's time to water when the condensation on the glass jar walls becomes less.

Death in Victorian England

Death is an underlying theme in The Secret Garden. Mary is sent back to England because of her parents' deaths in India. Colin's mother died by falling off a swing in the garden, leaving Colin to be raised by the household staff.

People in Victorian/Edwardian England died from many causes in those days. Illnesses such as scarlet fever, typhoid, cholera; burns from cooking; and childbirth played their part in the demise of many.

Queen Victoria, on the death of her husband Albert, set elaborate death and burial rituals to commemorate her husband. Society as a whole embraced these rituals, so that when someone passed away there was tradition and etiquette in place to follow.

"What would you like to wear?" asks Martha, "black, black, or black?"

"Are you blind?" snaps Mary, pointing at three identical dresses. "They're all black."

When a person died, the mourning period began immediately. Curtains were closed, clocks were stopped at the time of death, and mirrors were covered to keep the spirit of the deceased from being trapped in the reflective glass.

There were two types of mourning periods: deep mourning and half mourning.

Mourning clothes were worn to display the family's inner emotions and despair at losing a loved one. Deep mourning clothes were black. Women wore specific fabrics such as silk and crepe, while men work black gloves and black bands on their hats and cravats.

As the mourning period moved forward, clothes lightened from black to grey, then mauve, and finally white. When a mourner stopped wearing black, it was known as half mourning.

A widow mourned her husband for two years. She was expected to wear black and only go out for church services. Parents who lost their children were in full mourning for nine months and half mourning for three months. Children like Mary and Colin who lost their parents were in mourning for the same duration as a parent who lost a child. The death of a sibling required three months of deep mourning and three months of half mourning. Other family members such as in-laws, aunts, uncles, cousins, grandparents, etc., all had mourning periods that ranged from six weeks to six months.

Character Study: Archibald Craven

"She could see that the man in the chair was not so much a hunchback as a man with high, rather crooked shoulders, and he had black hair streaked with white…He was not ugly. His face would have been handsome if it had not been so miserable."

Lord Archibald Craven is the "hunchbacked" master of Misselthwaite Manor. He is father to Colin, brother to Mrs. Lennox, and uncle to Mary. He is a kind, caring man, but depression took hold of him after the death of his wife Lilias ten years before the novel takes place. He cannot bear to see his son, Colin, who resembles his wife so much. He spends as much time as possible away from Misselthwaite, leaving the house and estate in charge to Mrs. Medlock. At the end of the book, Archibald's wife comes to him in a dream; he returns to Misselthwaite to find his son in perfect health, and embraces him.

March

Sticky Toffee Pudding

INGREDIENTS

Pudding

- ¼ cup (½ stick) unsalted butter, room temperature, plus more for pan
- 1½ cups sifted all-purpose flour, plus more for pan
- 1½ cups chopped pitted dates (about 6 ounces)
- 1 teaspoon baking soda
- 1 teaspoon baking powder
- ½ teaspoon sea salt
- 1 cup sugar
- 1 teaspoon vanilla extract
- 2 large eggs

Sauce

- 1¼ cups (packed) light brown sugar
- ½ cup heavy cream
- ½ cup (½ stick) unsalted butter
- 1 teaspoon brandy (optional)
- ½ teaspoon vanilla extract
- Whipped cream or vanilla ice cream

SPECIAL EQUIPMENT

6-cup Bundt pan or 6 one-cup Bundt pan molds

[STICKY TOFFEE PUDDING, CONTINUED]

INSTRUCTIONS

Pudding

(Can be made 1 day ahead. Cover and let stand at room temperature.)

Preheat oven to 350°F (177ºC). Butter and flour Bundt pan. Bring dates and 1¼ cups water to a boil in a medium heavy saucepan with tall sides. Remove from heat; stir in baking soda (mixture will become foamy). Set aside; let cool.

Whisk 1½ cups flour, baking powder, and salt in a small bowl. Using an electric mixer, beat ¼ cup butter, sugar, and vanilla in a large bowl to blend (mixture will be grainy). Add 1 egg; beat to blend. Add half of flour mixture and half of date mixture; beat to blend. Repeat with remaining 1 egg, flour mixture, and date mixture. Pour batter into mold.

Bake until a tester inserted into center of cake comes out clean, 40–45 minutes. Let cool in pan on a wire rack for 30 minutes. Invert pudding onto rack.

Sauce

(Can be made 4 hours ahead. Let stand at room temperature. Rewarm gently before using.)

Bring sugar, cream, and butter to a boil in a small heavy saucepan over medium heat, stirring constantly. Continue to boil, stirring constantly, for 3 minutes. Remove from heat; stir in brandy, if using, and vanilla.

Cut cake into wedges. Serve with sauce and whipped cream.

Nest Building

"If you want to see birds, you must have birds in your heart."

— JOHN BURROUGHS

Finding a bird's nest in nature is a truly enchanting moment, but equally delightful is making a bird's nest of one's own.

COLLECTING WE WILL GO

It's time to grab your collecting bag and head outside to gather everything you'll need for your nest. A birds nest has two purposes: to support the bird and give it a place to rest, and to provide insulation and warmth. A bird makes hundreds of back-and-forth trips to gather the materials needed – you only have to take one wonderful walk. You might also want to hunt up some items from inside the house.

SUPPLIES AND GATHERINGS

- **Sticks, dried brush, pine needles, grass, moss, yarn, string, etc.**
- **A bowl (This is your nest mold)**
- **Plastic bag**
- **Clear Glue**
- **Heavy object such as a medium-sized river stone**

INSTRUCTIONS

Gather all of your nest items together.

Line your bowl with the plastic bag.

[NEST BUILDING, CONTINUED]

Using a circular pattern, lay down your twigs, brush, etc., being sure to overlap these items. You'll want to use your yarn pieces on the outside layer or the first layer to show some color in your nest.

Drizzle clear glue over everything.

Press down your nest so the glue spreads.

Do another layer using the same circular pattern as before.

Drizzle glue on everything.

Press down your nest so the glue spreads.

Once your nest has reached the thickness you'd like, weigh it down in the center with a heavy object such as a stone, a small ceramic bowl, or a baseball.

Let your nest sit overnight.

The next morning, turn your nest out of the bowl and let it sit for another 8 hours upside down.

After your nest is dry, line it with green moss if you want to.

Place your nest on a tree or bush outside. If you just can't give it up, put it on a shelf inside.

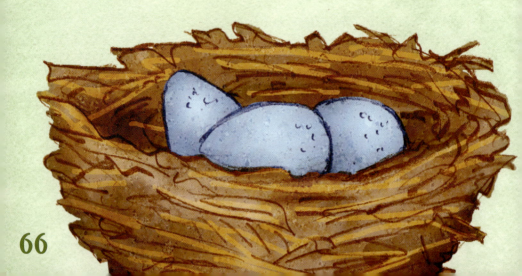

Seed Paper & Packets

Grow-Me Seed Paper

The mystery and magic of planting a seed and watching it grow is a very exciting experience indeed. Now imagine if you could put those seeds inside the fibers of a piece of paper to plant and watch your flowers grow. With this enchanting project you'll be able to amaze your friends.

SUPPLIES

- A few sheets of newspaper
- Scraps of colored paper
- A blender
- Water
- Towel or extra newspaper for drying
- Small, heart-shaped cookie cutter
- Plastic screen used in craft stitchery.
- Flower seeds – zinnias work well.
- Baking cooling rack

INSTRUCTIONS

Tear paper into nickel-sized pieces.

Soak the paper in water overnight. Put in enough water to cover all the paper.

Next day, place soaked paper into the blender.

Blend on high speed, occasionally stirring with a wooden spoon. Do not stir while blender is running.

If you want more color, add colored paper to your pulp blend.

After you have your pulp the color you'd like it, stir in your flower seeds by hand.

[GROW-ME SEED PAPER, CONTINUED]

Place a towel or newspaper under your screen.

Take your plastic screen and place your cookie cutter on top.

Take little bits of paper pulp and place them into the cookie cutter. Hold the cookie cutter in place and press the liquid out of the pulp.

Leave on a baking cooling rack to dry. Your seed paper may take a couple of days to dry completely.

Seed Packets

INSTRUCTIONS

Cut out packet and fold.

Glue tabs and let dry.

Fill with seeds for your Secret Garden.

Class of Hunger

In the Secret Garden, hunger plays an important role. It shows the well-being or stress of various characters, as well as where they live in the well-established British class system.

When Mary Lennox first arrives at her uncle's house Misselthwaite Manor, she is bad-tempered and a picky eater, showing how depressed and unhappy she is. As she spends more time outside in the garden, and her friendships with several characters in the story blossom, her appetite increases – a sign that she is growing healthier and happier.

Both Mary and Colin have access to a lot of food in the story. Often, we find them not eating their food so they can keep up the appearances of being sad and sickly. They don't want anyone in the house to know their secrets, both about the garden and their general well being. They talked often about sending food away but in the end they just couldn't.

At one point in the story, Mary and Collin spend so much time outdoors that they work up a ravenous appetite. Dickon's mom Susan Sowerby wards off their hunger by sending them fresh milk and bread.

The Sowerby family had 14 children in all. They had fresh milk and bread, but little else unless it came from the garden during the summer. This optimistic family would never send food away or pretend not to be hungry. Hunger was truly a part of their everyday life; they welcomed any food that came their way.

For Martha Sowerby, one of the perks of working as a servant at Misselthwaite Manor was food. She got to eat at least two meals a day.

For a majority of 19th-century England, hunger was a real issue. Though only a behind-the-scenes character in the Secret Garden, hunger is used as a symbol to show a return to health for main characters Mary and Colin.

Character Study : Colin Craven

"The boy had a sharp, delicate face, the colour of ivory and he seemed to have eyes too big for it. He had also a lot of hair which tumbled over his forehead in heavy locks and made his thin face seem smaller. He looked like a boy who had been ill, but he was crying more as if he were cross than as if he were in pain."

Colin Craven is the sickly, bed-ridden son of Lord Archibald Craven. He was born a very brief time before the death of his mother Lilias. Lord Craven refused to be with Colin because doing so reminded him constantly of his painful loss. It was expected that Colin would grow to have a hump like his father – he was therefore was treated like an invalid from birth.

Colin, believing that he is indeed an invalid, refuses to go out for fresh air and remains in his room watching the world from his bedroom window, dreading the day that he will finally die.

When Mary first encounters her cousin, Colin is certain that he is going to die. All the servants must answer his every whim – this makes him spoiled and arrogant. Colin is described as being like a Rajah – weak, hysterical, and fragile.

Mary helps Colin by contradicting his negative thinking and by not jumping at his every whim.

[COLIN CRAVEN, CONTINUED]

As the story unfolds, Mary and Dickon take Colin to the secret garden, where new ideas are planted in his head. Soon Colin is walking, and his gloomy sickness disappears. His greatest hope is to be connected to his father – at the end of the story they are reunited, and his father happily embraces him after finding him strong and well at last.

April

"The robin flew from his swinging spray of ivy on to the top of the wall and he opened his beak and sang a loud, lovely trill, merely to show off. Nothing in the world is quite as adorably lovely as a robin when he shows off – and they are nearly always doing it."

—Frances Hodgson Burnett,
The Secret Garden

The robin shows Mary the secret garden. In the month of April, Spring having just arrived, it's time to make robin cakes complete with a hidden chocolate egg inside and a lovely robin sitting on top.

Robin Cake

Equipment

Cupcake pan
Cupcake liners
Electric mixer

Ingredients

- **3 cups cake flour or 2½ cups all-purpose flour**
- **2 cups of sugar**
- **1 cup of butter**
- **1 cup of sour cream**
- **1 cup of water**
- **1¼ tsp baking soda**
- **¼ tsp baking powder**
- **1 tsp salt**
- **1 tsp of vanilla**
- **5 egg whites**
- **24 frozen Cadbury eggs**

Instructions

Preheat oven to 350ºF (177ºC)

Combine all of the ingredients together **except for the 5 egg whites and Cadbury eggs**. Beat with an electric mixer for 2 minutes to combine everything together.

In a separate bowl and with clean beaters, beat the egg whites at medium speed until stiff peaks form.

Gently fold egg whites into batter.

Place cupcake liners in cupcake pans.

Fill cupcake liners ¼–⅓ full

Place a frozen Cadbury egg thick side down inside the batter.

Cover the eggs with another 1–2 teaspoons of cake batter.

Bake for 19 minutes. Test your cupcakes with a toothpick to make sure they're done.

Buttercream Frosting

INGREDIENTS

- 1½ cups unsalted butter, slightly softened
- 2 lbs (907 g) sifted powdered sugar
- 1½ tsp vanilla extract
- ¼ tsp salt
- 2–3 tbsp milk

INSTRUCTIONS

In a stand mixer, mix butter and salt on medium speed until pale and smooth, about 5 mins. Scrape down sides of bowl.

Add powdered sugar one cup at a time, mixing on low after each addition. Scrape down sides of bowl.

Add vanilla and mix to combine.

Add 2–3 tablespoons of milk to reach the desired consistency of icing. Mix on low to blend after each addition.

Ice each cupcake in a circular motion.

[ROBIN CAKE, CONTINUED]

Dyeing Fondant Perfectly Every Time

Knead the fondant until it molds in your hands.

Roll it into a ball.

Dust the counter with powdered sugar.

Place ball on powdered sugar and make a little dip into the fondant for the dye to sit in.

[This next part goes for both brown and red dye.]

Start off with six drops of brown dye and knead into the fondant.

Put 4 to 5 drops of dye onto the outside of the fondant ball and then a few drops of dye onto your hands.

Knead until you achieve the desired color. Please feel free to add more dye color to the fondant as you see fit.

The Robins

INGREDIENTS

- 1 lb (454 g) white fondant icing
- Brown and red food coloring
- Powdered sugar for dusting
- Jar of cloves

INSTRUCTIONS

Roll a walnut sized ball of brown fondant for the body. Roll a smaller brown ball for the head. If need be, rub a little water on the bottom of the head to help it stick to the body.

Take a little clove and poke it into the robin's head for the beak.

Poke in the eyes with a skewer or toothpick.

Tear off a small piece of red fondant and mold it into a tear drop.

Dab a little water on the back and add it to the body with the point facing downward. This is the robin's red breast.

For the finishing touches, pinch the back of the body to make a little tail. Then take the round part off the cloves and use them as feet.

Stick them on top of your Robin Cakes.

Dickon's Felt Creatures

Dickon is a magical boy who can tame and speak to the animals. Wherever he goes so do the creatures he adores. We all need a little creature comfort – here are three to make of your own.

CUT 2

CUT 2

Fox

CUT 2

CUT 2

Lamb

[MORE OF DICKON'S FELT CREATURES]

Rabbit

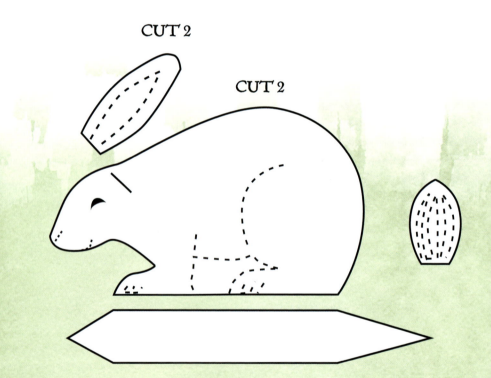

The World of Mason Bees

Keeping non-stinging mason bees is a great way to help the environment. Mason bees are especially beneficial to both flowers and fruit trees. Unlike other types of bees, mason bees don't live in hives but make their nests inside hollow stems, woodpecker drillings, and other insect holes found in wood. Mason bees however live a solitary life – they neither share their nests, protect each other or one another's young, nor share food. Mason bees are only active for a few weeks a year and are not aggressive. Though mason bees are great pollinators, they unfortunately do not produce honey.

Making a Mason Bee House

Mason bees oftentimes make their nests near each other, just as long as each bee has it's own tube.

SUPPLIES

- **Medium-sized flowerpot**
- **Paint and paintbrush,** if you're painting your flowerpot
- **Cardboard-colored brown card stock**
- **Ruler**
- **Pencil**
- **Wooden spoon**
- **Tape**
- **Scissors**

PREPARING THE CONTAINER

Make sure your container is dry and clean.

Plug the drainage hole.

If you're painting the outside of your container, use a bright color such as yellow. Mason bees love bright colors.

[MASON BEE HOUSE, CONTINUED]

MAKING NESTING TUBES

Cut the brown card stock into 6-1/4" × 5" pieces.

Wrap each piece of card stock around the end of a wooden spoon. Secure it with a few small pieces of tape. Close one end of the tube with tape as well. Slide the spoon out of the paper tube.

Assemble the bee house by placing each nesting tube inside the flower pot, open end facing out.

Keep adding nesting tubes until the container is full.

Place the mason bee house outside, close to the house or out in the garden near bushes and flowers.

British Money

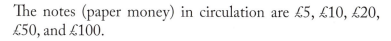

Since 1971, the monetary system of Great Britain has been based on the decimal system. The basic unit of British currency is the pound, which is divided into one hundred pence.

The coins in circulation are 1 penny, 2 pence, 5 pence, 10 pence, 20 pence, 50 pence, 1 pound, 2 pounds.

The notes (paper money) in circulation are £5, £10, £20, £50, and £100.

Old British Money

Prior to decimalization in 1971, Britain used a system of pounds, shillings and pence. This is the money system used in the time period of The Secret Garden. The smallest unit of currency is a penny, the plural of which is pence (or pennies). There are 12 pence in a shilling and 20 shillings in a pound. The pound is either a paper bill, called a note, or a gold coin, called a sovereign.

1 farthing (the lowest value coin) = ¼ penny

A ha'penny (half penny – a copper coin) = ½ penny (pronounced "heipni")

1 penny (a copper coin) = one of the basic units (1d)

Threepence or thruppenny bit = 3 pence (pronounced "thruppence")

Sixpence (a silver coin also called a 'tanner') = 6 pence

1 shilling = 12 pence (1s)

1 florin (a silver coin that numismatists regard as one of the most beautiful medieval English coins) = 2 shillings

A half-crown = 2½ shillings = 30 pence = ⅛ pound

[More British Money]

1 crown = 5 shillings = ¼ pound

1 pound = 20 shillings = 240 pence (£1)

1 sovereign = a gold coin with a face value of 20 shillings, or one pound (about .24 ounces of 22 carat gold)

1 guinea = another gold coin, worth 21 shillings

Farthings were not produced after 1956, and were withdrawn in 1960 because of inflation. In preparation for decimalization, the ha'penny was withdrawn in 1969, and the half-crown withdrawn the year after.

A penny was often called a copper after the metal it was minted from.

The old slang term for a shilling was 'bob,' and for a guinea, 'yellow-boy.'

Other Slang Terms:

fiver = £5, Lady Godiva (Cockney rhyming slang)

tenner = £10

pony = £25

half a ton = £50

ton = £100

monkey = £500

grand = £1000

Character Study: Dr. Craven

Dr. Craven is Archibald's brother who tends to Colin. He has an interest in Colin not getting well – if Colin should die, it is he who would inherit Misselthwaite Manor. We do not hear a lot about him in the story, but he is clearly an ally of Mrs. Medlock.

May

"And the secret garden bloomed and bloomed and every morning revealed new miracles."

—Frances Hodgson Burnett, The Secret Garden

Country gardens are blooming everywhere with old fashioned tulips, hollyhocks and sweet peas. Roses climb over the garden walls while scented geraniums, chives, and strawberries spill onto the paths and peek out from the borders.

When we see the strawberries go red, we know it's time to go strawberry picking so that we can make some of our favorite jam. Though some jam is put away in jars for winter use, our frozen strawberry jam can't seem to wait. It's all gone as quickly as I can make it.

Freezer Strawberry Jam

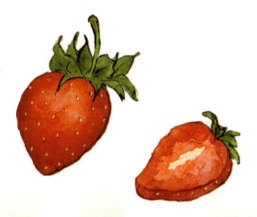

INGREDIENTS

2 cups crushed fresh strawberries

4 cups sugar

1 (1.75 oz) package dry pectin

¾ cup water

INSTRUCTIONS

Crush strawberries with a potato masher, or on pulse in a food processor

Mix crushed strawberries with the sugar and let stand for 10 minutes.

While you're waiting for the berries to juice up, stir the pectin into the water in a saucepan.

Bring water to a boil over medium-high heat. Boil for 1 minute.

Stir the boiling water into the strawberries.

Let stand for 3 minutes before pouring into freezer containers.

Place tops on containers and leave standing at room temperature for 24 hours.

Place into freezer and store frozen until ready to use. Freezer jam is good in the freezer for 6 months.

Planting a Rose Bush

*"Where you tend a rose my lad,
a thistle cannot grow."*

FRANCES HODGSON BURNETT,
THE SECRET GARDEN

One of the first flowers peeking over the wall of the secret garden were roses. Nothing makes a garden more appealing than the beautiful fragrance, colors, and shape of roses.

HOW TO PLANT A ROSE BUSH

First of all, it is very important to choose a sunny area of the garden that gets at least 4 to 5 hours of sun for your rose. Do not crowd your rose with other trees and plants. Some roses, such as climbers and shrubs, don't mind company, but most roses like to mix with other roses or other non-invasive plants.

ROSE PLANTING BASICS

Dig a hole slightly larger than the pot size or root system of your rose bush.

Add a small handful of bone meal to the planting hole. Spade in some compost or peat moss to loosen the soil. Mix the soil you took out of the hole with more compost or peat moss.

Remove the rose from the pot. Carefully place in the hole and shovel the extra soil around the new plant. Plant the rose with the crown slightly deeper than the original soil. The crown or bud union should be about 1 inch under the soil.

Gently firm the rose into its new home and water well.

Stand back and watch it grow!

Important note!! NEVER fertilize a new rose bush with anything other than bone meal.

If you have received bare-root bushes from a mail order nursery, soak them in a bucket of water for a few hours before planting. If you have purchased your roses in containers, you do not have to pre-soak them before planting.

Wheelbarrow Race

Play this game with four or more players outside or in an open area.

To play, find a partner and decide who will be the wheelbarrow first.

To make a wheelbarrow, get down on all fours. Have your partner stand behind you and lift up your legs while you support yourself with your hands.

To Race

Mark a starting line and a finish line.

Have all teams line up at the starting line.

Get in position. On the word 'go', race the other teams to the finish line. The team that gets there first wins.

For a variation, race to the finish line, switch partners, and race back to the starting line.

Spot-Sitting

"O, the green things growing, the green things growing, the faint sweet smell of the green things growing."

—Dinah Mulock Craik

A sit spot is a place all your own to return to day after day, season after season. A sit spot isn't a shared space but a place to be by yourself, and attentively present. Spot-sitting is a practice of observation.

There aren't a lot of rules.

Discover a place nearby which feels like it is calling to you; a place you feel a connection with.

Spend some time there every day. A half-hour is great, but 15 minutes will do. Make sure you go there during different times of the day. A true added bonus is the nighttime view.

While you are in your special place, take notice of what types of plants are there. What color are they? What do their leaves look like? See any bugs? Close your eyes. What do you hear? What do you feel? Just sit quiet and be still for a moment.

When you feel like getting up, do so. Do you want to collect any items? Do you feel like making a fort from sticks? Do what feels right to you, but please remember to be a caretaker of your special place.

At first you may feel nervous or fearful. That's OK. What's making you feel nervous or frightened? When you can identify what's making you frightened, you can learn about that issue and grow from it. Remember that the more you get to know about your sitting spot, the more it will become a good friend to you.

[SPOT SITTING, CONTINUED]

It is important to wear the correct clothing. My mother always said, "There is no such thing as bad weather, just bad clothing." Dress appropriately for all seasons and have a great time.

Many people who spot-sit like to bring a journal with them to write down their observations. This is a great way to see how the seasons change day by day.

Share with your family all of the wonderful things you have discovered. These moments in special places lend to wonderful conversations for all involved.

Character Study: Lilias Craven

Lilias was Archibald's wife and Colin's mother. She died ten years before the start of the novel by falling from a tree in her garden. She is described as beautiful and gentle. It is because Colin looks so much like his mother that it is unbearable for Lord Craven to be with him. Colin has a painting of his mother hanging behind a curtain. It bothers him, mostly because she is always smiling. As he comes to terms with her death, the curtain over the painting remains open, and as he takes care of the Secret Garden, memories of her become his greatest blessing.

June

Fireflies are flickering, flowers are blooming, and June 21st is the longest day of the year, known as Midsummer. Fire, food, and fairies make midsummer a magical time to spend in the garden with family and friends.

"Don't sleep away the long days of summer."

A Midsummer Garden Tea Party

Afternoon tea is a mini-meal between lunch and dinner. It evolved as an afternoon ritual during the reign of Queen Victoria.

Though many fine hotels serve high tea in the afternoon, bringing out all of the best china and silver service, high tea in England literally means taking tea sitting in high chairs; taking tea in low chairs would be considered having "low tea."

A garden tea party is always a special affair, with many people invited. What better way to celebrate Midsummer than having a garden tea party?

[A Midsummer Garden Tea Party, continued]

Tea parties look elegant, but the most important part is to have fun, enticing food. There is a wide variety of tea party food such as scones with marmalade and Devonshire cream, lemon curd, little sandwiches, miniature chocolate éclairs, lemon squares, milk cake, chocolate-covered strawberries, and butter cookies.

Pull out the china teapot and teacups, silver spoons and linen napkins, and get started by making these yummy treats for your garden party:

Ladybug Sandwiches

INGREDIENTS

- **15 thin slices of baguette**
- **¼ cup of fat free sour cream**
- **¼ cup of crumbled feta cheese**
- **1 green onion**
- **8 cherry tomatoes**
- **8 large pitted black olives**
- **1 slice of lettuce, cut to size**

INSTRUCTIONS

Finely chop the onions.

Mix together the onions, sour cream, and feta cheese.

Place the baguette slices on a tray and place in the oven under the broiler for a couple of minutes.

Spread ½ tablespoon of the sour cream mixture on each slice of bread.

Tear the lettuce leaves a bit smaller than the baguette slices.

Place the lettuce pieces on top of the baguette slices.

Cut the olives and tomatoes in half lengthwise.

Cut the tomatoes from one end to the middle of the tomato.

Cut the olive halves into thirds, width wise. These will make the heads of the ladybugs.

Using a knife with a sharp point, make 4 tiny holes in the tomatoes, 2 on each side.

Cut small pieces from the remainder of the olives, and place them in the little tomato holes.

Taking the ladybug head, make two small holes for the eyes. Fill with small bits of feta cheese.

Place tomatoes on top of the lettuce leaves.

Add the olive slices for the head in front of the tomato.

Place ladybug slices on a platter and serve.

Rainbow Fruit Kabobs

INGREDIENTS

- **Red grapes**
- **Blueberries**
- **Strawberry halves**
- **Green grapes**
- **One can of pineapple chunks or triangles**
- **Cantaloupe cut into small squares**

INSTRUCTIONS

On a bamboo skewer, place the fruit in the following order:

Red grape – blueberry – green grape – pineapple chunk – cantaloupe square – strawberry half

Simply Divine Lemon Cookies

INGREDIENTS

- **1 package of lemon cake mix**
- **2 eggs**
- **⅓ cup vegetable oil**
- **1 tsp pure lemon extract**
- **⅓ powdered sugar for decoration**

INSTRUCTIONS

Preheat oven to 375ºF (190ºC)

Pour cake mix into a large bowl. Stir in eggs, oil, and lemon extract.

Blend well.

Drop teaspoonfuls of dough into a bowl of powdered sugar.

Roll them around until they're lightly covered.

Once sugared, put them on an ungreased cookie sheet.

Bake for 8–10 minutes. The bottoms will be light brown.

Transfer to a wire rack to cool.

Daisy Chain Crowns

The fields and beds are crowded with blooming flowers everywhere. Daisy chain crowns are easy to make, and let you look festive and summery.

SUPPLIES

5–10 daisies, any color. Make sure that the daisies you choose are short and have thick stems. Daisies should be fully open.

INSTRUCTIONS

Make a small incision near the base of the stem with your thumbnail, but don't split the stem all the way to the bottom. The slit should be a bit longer than the thickness of the next daisy stem.

Thread the stem of another daisy through the slit.

Continue this process until your daisy chain is long enough to go around your head when made into a circle.

When your daisy chain is long enough, thread the stem of the last daisy into a slit at the top of the first daisy.

Midsummer Dancing Ribbon Wreaths

The sun is shining with a light fragrant breeze; get ready to celebrate midsummer with dance and song! Ribbon wreaths are fun to hold while dancing and running around.

SUPPLIES

- Small grapevine wreath or grapevines you can make into a small wreath
- 4 colors of ribbon, 1 yard each
- Thread or twine
- Scissors
- Needle and thread if you decide to sew the ribbons on

INSTRUCTIONS

If using grapevines, make into a small wreath. Tie it off with thread or twine.

Cut two 18-inch strips from each ribbon color.

Tie or sew the end of each ribbon onto the wreath.

Flower Pressing

Pressing flowers is a great way to preserve a bit of summer. Take a walk into nature and gather flowers, leaves, herb branches or anything that catches your eye.

Bring along a basket you can lay your collected flowers in.

When you get back home, put your flowers in a glass of water if they look a little limp. Be sure not to get the petals wet.

Remove the flowers from the water and pat them dry with a paper towel. If you press your flowers wet, they will get moldy.

Place coffee filters or newspaper in the middle of a big book.

Place your flowers face down on the filters/paper. Feel free to position the petals of your flowers.

Place a second filter or sheet of paper on top.

Close the book and stack three or four books on top of the book with the flowers in it.

Leave your flowers in the book for 2–4 weeks to make sure they are fully pressed and dried.

> *"I am the Sun –*
> *And I bear with my might*
> *The earth by day, the earth by night.*
> *I hold her fast, and my gifts I bestow*
> *To everything on her, so that it may grow:*
> *Man and stone, flower and bee*
> *All receive their light from me.*
> *Open thy heart like a little flower,*
> *That with my light I may thee dower:*
> *Open thy heart, dear child, to me,*
> *That we together one light may be."*
>
> —CHRISTIAN MORGENSTERN

Character Study: Victorian/Edwardian Family Life

Family life was very important in Victorian/Edwardian England. Each member of the family had his or her own place, and children especially were taught to know theirs.

The Father

The father was the head of the household. He was often strict and was obeyed by all without question. The children were taught to respect their father and always spoke politely to him, calling him "Sir." Very few children would dare to talk back to their fathers or be rude in any way. When he wanted a little peace and quiet, he would retire to his study, and the rest of the family were not allowed to enter without his special permission.

The Mother

The mother would often spend her time planning dinner parties, visiting her dressmaker, or calling on friends. She did not do jobs like washing clothes or cooking and cleaning. Both the mother and father saw the upbringing of their children as an important responsibility. They believed a child must be taught the difference between right and wrong if he was to grow into a good and thoughtful adult. If a child did something wrong, he would be punished for his own good. "Spare the rod and spoil the child" was a saying Victorians firmly believed in.

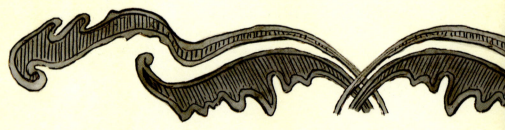

CHILDREN

Most days, upper and middle class children saw very little of their parents. The children spent most of their time in the nursery and were brought up by their nanny. Victorian children were expected to rise early because lying in bed was thought to be lazy and sinful. The nanny was paid about £25 a year to wash, dress, and watch over them, amuse them, give them medicine when it was needed, take them out, and teach them how to behave. Some children would only see their parents once a day. In the evening, the children, clean and tidy, were allowed downstairs for an hour before they went to bed.

Some mothers taught their children to read and write, and sometimes fathers taught their sons Latin. As the children grew older, tutors and governesses were often employed, and boys were sometimes sent away to school

When the children grew up, only the boys were expected to work or maintain their estates. The daughters stayed at home with their mother or were married off as soon as they came of age.

POOR AND WORKING CLASS FAMILIES

Poorer families' greatest fear was ending up in the workhouse, where thousands of homeless and penniless families were forced to live. If your family was taken into the workhouse, you were split up, dressed in uniforms, and had your hair cut short. This sometimes happened to a family if the father was sick and unable to work.

Lots of children in poor families died of diseases like scarlet fever, measles, polio, and tuberculosis, which are preventable today. These were spread by foul drinking water, open drains, and lack of clean toilets. Rooms were often overcrowded; if one person caught a disease, it spread quickly through the rest.

July

The Secret Meal

"Dickon made the stimulating discovery that in the wood in the park outside the garden where Mary had first found him piping to the wild creatures there was a deep little hollow where you could build a sort of tiny oven with stones and roast potatoes and eggs in it. Roasted eggs were a previously unknown luxury and very hot potatoes with salt and fresh butter in them were fit for a woodland king – besides being deliciously satisfying. You could buy both potatoes and eggs and eat as many as you liked without feeling as if you were taking food out of the mouths of fourteen people."

—Frances Hodgson Burnett, The Secret Garden

Wouldn't scrambled eggs and potatoes cooked on an open-fire on the moor be delicious? Here's a camping version which can be made on a camp-fire, a camping cook-stove, or barbecue.

Tin Foil Breakfast

Makes enough for 1 person per foil package.

INGREDIENTS

- **hash brown potatoes**
- **1–2 eggs**
- **1 sausage link (optional)**
- **salt and pepper**
- **aluminum Foil**
- **cooking spray**

INSTRUCTIONS

Tear off a piece of aluminum foil large enough to hold your eggs and potatoes.

Spray the non-shiny surface of your foil with cooking spray.

Break eggs into a bowl and beat them until well mixed.

Place potatoes, beaten eggs (uncooked), sausage, and salt and pepper to taste in the aluminum foil.

Wrap securely.

Place on hot white coals for approximately 15 minutes.

Turn and rotate as needed.

The Cooking Campfire

First Things First! Fire Safety

- **NEVER** build your fire near tents or other flammable items.
- **NEVER** use flammable fluids to start your fire.
- **NEVER** leave your fire unattended.
- Have a bucket of water, shovel, and fire extinguisher nearby, ready to put out a fire
- Build your fire only as big as you need.

Elements Required For A Fire To Burn Properly

When one of these three things are removed, the fire stops burning. Some examples: water cools the fuel below ignition point, dirt cuts off the oxygen supply.

- **Fuel** – material that will burn
- **Heat** – enough heat to bring fuel to ignition
- **Air** – to provide oxygen to burning process

Before You Light It

Clear area of all debris. Avoid areas with overhanging branches.

Construct a fire ring surrounded by rocks.

Gather wood and stack in separate piles away from fire area. Do not use green or freshly cut wood. There are three different kinds of wood needed for a successful campfire:

- **Tinder** – small twigs, wood shavings, dry leaves or grass, dry needles, bark, or dryer lint. Tinder should start to burn immediately with a lighted match.
- **Kindling** – small sticks, one inch around or smaller
- **Fuel** – larger wood that keeps the fire going

Building the Fire

Start with a couple hands full of tinder loosely piled in the center of your fire ring.

With your back to the wind and match protected by your cupped hand, ignite tinder with a match. Discard used match into the fire.

Slowly add more tinder. You may need to blow softly at the base of the fire.

Once the tinder has fully started to burn, slowly add some smaller pieces of kindling. Keep them close together, but allow space for air.

Gradually increase the size of the kindling you add to the fire.

When you have a good fire going, add the fuel one piece at a time as described below. Allow for adequate air flow.

Types of fires:

- **Tepee Fire** – good for quick cooking since the heat is concentrated in one spot. Lay the fuel over your kindling like a tepee.
- **Crisscross Fire** – good for a long lasting fire with a lot of coals. Excellent for a campfire. Lay the fuel over the kindling in a crisscross pattern.

[The Cooking Campfire, continued]

When You're Done

Make sure to completely extinguish your fire.

Scatter ashes or embers out.

Sprinkle with water. Stir with a stick.

Drench charred logs.

Repeat until everything is cold.

Creating a Garden Journal

A garden journal is great for writing down, drawing, and saving any little discoveries you make while out in the garden. You can bring a little bit of nature to the journal itself by using a stick for its spine.

SUPPLIES:

- **Several pieces of heavy paper such as #80 weight or drawing paper.**
- **A strong rubber band.**
- **A straight stick about 8 to 10 inches long.**
- **Scissors**
- **Glue**

INSTRUCTIONS

Place a few pages in a neat stack and fold them in half. You don't want your paper stack too thick or you won't be able to cut through it.

With your pages folded, cut 2 triangular notches, two inches from each end.

Line the stick up with the spine.

Slip the rubber band over one end of the stick and slide it down to the first notch.

Keeping the rubber band on the stick, slip the end of the rubber band through the notch.

Along the inside fold, stretch the rubber band down the journal's spine and pull the end out through the other notch, slipping it over the other end of the stick. This is a temporary binding to hold the journal together.

Decorate the cover of your journal anyway you'd like to.

Colin's Exercises

Each time Colin goes into the secret garden he creates a ritual, doing the same thing every time. Calisthenics, or exercises, are part of his ritual. Aided by the fresh air of the great outdoors, Colin recovers from his illness by doing physical exercise to increase his healthy disposition.

In 1910, when this book was written, gym exercises were very different than they are now. Remember that people wore constrictive clothing that made it difficult to move freely and easily.

A fun article in a women's magazine written on March 13th, 1910, states the importance of mothers exercising their children, and offers these instructions:

Exercise 1: The Waist

Bend over and touch your toes – or better yet, the floor – with your hands. Come back up and bring your hands over your head, then bend down again to touch the floor. Do this 10 times.

Exercise 2: The Legs

Lift your knee up into a right angle, then set it back down on the floor/ground. Do this on each leg 10 times

Exercise 3: Deep Breathing

Straighten your arms out in front of your body, taking a deep breath in. Extend your arms out to your sides like airplane wings, and exhale as your arms move. Bring your arms back in front of your body taking a deep breath in. Do this 10 times.

Blindfolded Garden Walk

So much of what we observe in the natural world is via our sight. Experiencing the same environment while blindfolded opens up the other senses of hearing, smell, and touch. Closing down our most dominant sense intensifies the others.

Blindfolded, you'll smell the dampness of the forest, hear the blowing or crunching of the leaves, feel the sun or shade, and notice what type of ground you're walking on. You'll have a new perception of the world.

SUPPLIES

Anything usable as a blindfold – scarves, eye-shades, bandanas.

INSTRUCTIONS

Have a walk or trail planned out ahead of time.

Make sure when preparing the route that there are not too many obstacles.

Tell the guides to watch out for logs, branches, exposed roots, or anything poisonous such as snakes, spiders, or poison ivy or oak.

[BLINDFOLDED GARDEN WALK, CONTINUED]

Organize the children into pairs. One child will be blindfolded and the other will be the guide.

Have guides try some of these things with their blindfolded partners:

Point out natural objects to them: bark, stones, moss, lichen, etc.

Crush different herbs and flowers under their noses to see if they can guess what it is.

Let them feel different shapes and textures such as acorns, leaves, feathers, pinecones, etc.

Lead them over different surfaces such as grass, brick or stone paths, sand, mud, and puddles to give a wide variety of textures to feel with their feet.

Colin's Magic Chant and Affirmations

As the story of the secret garden unfolds, both Mary and Colin blossom from sad, grumpy children into content, happy people who believe in "white magic" in the garden; "White magic" being the special, extraordinary moments in life that are good and all-encompassing. When Colin saw the secret garden in full bloom, he was excited and awestruck:

> *"Of course there must be lots of Magic in the world,"* he said wisely one day, *"but people don't know what it is like or how to make it. Perhaps the beginning is just to say nice things are going to happen until you make them happen. I am going to try and experiment."...*
>
> *Colin really looked quite beautiful, Mary thought. He held his head high as if he felt like a sort of priest and his strange eyes had a wonderful look in them. The light shone on him through the tree canopy.*
>
> *"Now we will begin," he said. "Shall we sway backward and forward, Mary, as if we were dervishes?"*
>
> *"I canna' do no swayin' back'ard and for'ard," said Ben Weatherstaff. "I've got th' rheumatics."*
>
> *"The Magic will take them away," said Colin in a High Priest tone, "but we won't sway until it has done it. We will only chant."*
>
> *"I canna' do no chantin'" said Ben Weatherstaff a trifle testily. "They turned me out o' th' church choir th' only time I ever tried it."*

[COLIN'S MAGIC CHANT, CONTINUED]

No one smiled. They were all too much in earnest. Colin's face was not even crossed by a shadow. He was thinking only of the Magic.

"Then I will chant," he said. And he began, looking like a strange boy spirit. "The sun is shining – the sun is shining. That is the Magic. The flowers are growing – the roots are stirring. That is the Magic. Being alive is the Magic – being strong is the Magic. The Magic is in me – the Magic is in me. It is in me – it is in me. It's in every one of us. It's in Ben Weatherstaff's back. Magic! Magic! Come and help!"

—FRANCES HODGSON BURNETT, *THE SECRET GARDEN*

Author Frances Hodgson Burnett truly believed that by changing the way you think about something, you can change the outcome. It's known as "You are what you think". She wove this deeply-held belief into The Secret Garden: Both Mary and Colin have a metamorphosis from depressed, angry children to inspired, creative, and happy ones.

In Colin's chant, he uses something which is called an affirmation. An affirmation is something positive you say, think, or feel about yourself. In the beginning of the story, Colin thinks he is sick, will develop a lump on his back like his father, and ultimately die – when he tells himself that he wants to get well, that he wants to walk and be able to go outside and discover the wonders of the world like his cousin Mary, that is a positive affirmation.

What you think, you become. It's as Colin says, "The magic is in me."

Affirmation Stones

Affirmations work for everyone. Carrying a little stone inscribed with a positive thought is a way to stir the magic in you.

Rock and Stone Search

Take a walk with a heavy, durable basket or other container. Pick 10–20 medium to large stones; the size of the palm of your hand or a little larger.

SUPPLIES

- Heavy-bottomed basket or other container
- Affirmation sheet
- Scissors
- Mod Podge
- Small paint brush

INSTRUCTIONS

Wash and dry the stones.

Cut out the affirmations you want to use from the printable affirmation sheet (below).

Spread glue on the back of your affirmation.

Stick the affirmation to your rock, wrapping it around if necessary.

Make any adjustments needed to the affirmation's position, then brush mod podge on top of it.

Place your rock(s) on a cookie sheet to dry.

Once they're dry, place all of the affirmation stones in a basket or other container.

[AFFIRMATION STONES, CONTINUED]

CHOOSING AFFIRMATION STONES

Place the stones in a basket. Close your eyes and pick one. Carry that stone with you throughout the day or place it in a visible area where you can see your affirmation. Repeat your affirmation to yourself often.

Alternatively, go through the basket and find the affirmation that feels right for you. Carry it with you in your pocket. Look at it often and repeat the affirmation to yourself.

Before bed, look at your affirmation stone one more time, then return it to the affirmation basket.

AFFIRMATION PHRASES

1. I can do whatever I focus my mind on.
2. I am awesome.
3. I am very intelligent.
4. I am a fast learner.
5. I am worthy.
6. I deeply love and accept myself.
7. I enjoy learning.
8. Learning is fun and exciting.
9. I understand the lessons taught in school completely and quickly.
10. I believe in myself and my abilities.
11. While I appreciate details, I am also able to see the big picture.
12. I have many gifts and talents.
13. I learn from my challenges and can always find ways to overcome them.
14. I am open to possibility.

15. I embrace my fears fully and calmly.
16. I make like-minded friends easily and naturally.
17. I am healthy and am growing up well.
18. I have persistence in what I believe in.
19. Miracles happen to me all the time.
20. I am very creative.
21. Ideas for problem solving come easily and quickly to me.
22. I am a great listener.
23. My family, friends, and teachers love me for who I am.
24. I am unique and special.
25. Opportunities come to me in good time.
26. I make mistakes sometimes, but I choose to learn from them.
27. I accept myself even though I sometimes make mistakes.
28. Every day and in every way, I get better and better.
29. My intuition guides me in what I do.
30. I am calm, relaxed, and peaceful.
31. I am always in the right place at the right time.
32. I enjoy being, feeling, and thinking positive.
33. Problems challenge me to better myself in every way.
34. I trust myself in making great decisions.
35. I am loving kindness to all.
36. I do my best in my work and tasks.
37. I am present.
38. I trust in my ability to solve problems.
39. I enjoy my own company.
40. I accept compliments graciously and openly.
41. I am whole and complete.
42. I enjoy trying new ideas.

[AFFIRMATION STONES, CONTINUED]

43. I embrace changes in peaceful, harmonious and positive ways.
44. I can be whatever I want to be.
45. I visualize very well.
46. I am vibrant and have lots of energy.
47. I am divinely protected.
48. I am kind, generous, and loving.
49. I complete my schoolwork on time every day.
50. I deserve love, trust, and kindness.
51. I achieve great and successful results.
52. I am brave.
53. I experience beauty wherever I go.
54. I have an awesome imagination.
55. I solve problems creatively.
56. All is well in the world.
57. I am thankful for my blessings.
58. I have a healthy relationship with my teachers.
59. I forgive all others for any mistakes they have made.
60. I am confident and secure.
61. I enjoy letting events unfold in good time.
62. I have loving, positive, and happy thoughts.
63. I express my ideas easily.
64. I am courageous even when things are unknown to me.
65. I reach my goals easily.
66. I am in charge of my own life.
67. I enjoy playing games with my friends.
68. I am gentle with myself.
69. I have many friends who like being near me.

70. The trees, flowers, and birds are my friends.
71. I radiate love and compassion.
72. Miracles happen to me every day.
73. I am on my way to creating great wealth.
74. I am excellent with languages.
75. I am quick and accurate with Mathematics.
76. I am able to analyze and see clearly when problem-solving.
77. I read, write, and learn fast.
78. I absorb knowledge like a sponge and apply what I learn.
79. I do my best in my studies.
80. I am attentive in class.

[AFFIRMATION STONES, CONTINUED]

81. I am a natural at _____ (sports/music/art/etc.).
82. I am on top of my classes.
83. I enjoy challenging myself with new ideas, possibilities, and directions.
84. I am a winner!
85. I turn failures into opportunities for success.
86. I handle all my responsibilities and tasks well.
87. I eat healthy snacks.
88. I love my body.
89. I am honest and trustworthy.
90. I look for the best way forward for myself.
91. I understand and solve complex problem sums or questions easily.
92. I experience life in multiple ways.
93. I love being healthy!
94. I manage my time well.
95. I am punctual.
96. I have habits that will help me have a happy, healthy, and successful life.
97. I listen closely to my gut or inner wisdom.
98. I easily draw inspiration from nature and life.
99. I believe in my dreams.
100. I have an excellent memory.

Character Study: Susan Sowerby

Living in a very crowded cottage five miles from the estate, Susan Sowerby is the mother of no less than twelve children, including Martha and Dickon. She is the perfect symbol of motherhood. Just as Dickon knows everything there is to know about the moor and its hoard of animals, Susan Sowerby knows all there is to know about children. She is bold and kind, and both Mary and Colin become fascinated with her simply by listening to the stories Dickon and Martha tell. It is not until near the very end of the story that Colin and Mary finally get to meet her and feel her embrace and motherly love.

August

"At first people refuse to believe that a strange new thing can be done, then they begin to hope it can be done, then they see it can be done – then it is done and all the world wonders why it was not done centuries ago."

—Frances Hodgson Burnett

Scones and Ginger Tea

Ingredients

- 2 cups all-purpose flour
- ½ cup sugar
- 2 teaspoons baking powder
- ¼ cup cold butter, cubed
- 1 cup raisins
- ½ cup milk
- 1 egg
- Additional milk

Instructions

In a large bowl, combine the flour, sugar, and baking powder. Cut in butter until mixture resembles fine crumbs. Stir in raisins. Beat milk and egg; add to dry ingredients, stirring gently.

Turn onto a lightly floured surface; roll to 1-inch thickness. Cut with a 2½-inch biscuit cutter. Bake at 425°F (220ºC) for 10–15 minutes or until golden brown. Serve warm. Makes 10 scones.

A Taste of Summer

(Fruit- and Herb-Infused Water)

This is an easy way to make something refreshing to drink. It's simply summer in a jar.

SUPPLIES

- 2-quart pitcher or jar with a lid
- Wooden spoon

INGREDIENTS

fruit – 2 cups berries, citrus, melons, pineapple; most fruits will work (see recommended amounts in directions)

herbs – a sprig of mint, basil, sage, rosemary, tarragon, thyme, or lavender

water (tap or filtered)

ice

[A Taste of Summer, continued]

Instructions

Here is a general formula to use with whatever fruit/herb combo you desire:

> If using herbs, add a sprig of fresh herbs to jar/pitcher; press and twist with muddler or handle of wooden spoon to bruise leaves and release flavor; don't pulverize the herbs into bits.
>
> Add approximately 2 cups of fruit to jar/pitcher; press and twist with muddler or handle of wooden spoon just enough to release some of the juices
>
> Fill jar/pitcher with ice cubes.
>
> Add water to top of jar/pitcher.
>
> Cover and refrigerate for up to 3 days.

Favorite Combinations:

Citrus: Slice 1 orange, 1 lime, and 1 lemon into rounds, then cut the rounds in half. Add to jar and stir; add ice and water.

Raspberry Lime: Quarter 2 limes; with your hands, squeeze the juice into the jar, then throw in the squeezed lime quarters. Add 2 cups raspberries. Stir, add ice and water.

Pineapple Mint: Add a sprig of mint to the jar (you can throw in the whole sprig; or, remove the leaves from the sprig, if you prefer to have the mint swimming around and distributing in the jar). Stir the mint. Add 2 cups pineapple pieces, stir, add ice and water.

Blackberry Sage: Add sage sprig to jar and stir. Add 2 cups blackberries; stir, add ice and water.

Watermelon Rosemary: Add rosemary sprig to jar and stir. Add 2 cups watermelon cubes; stir, add ice and water.

Paper Garden Model

[Paper Garden Model, continued]

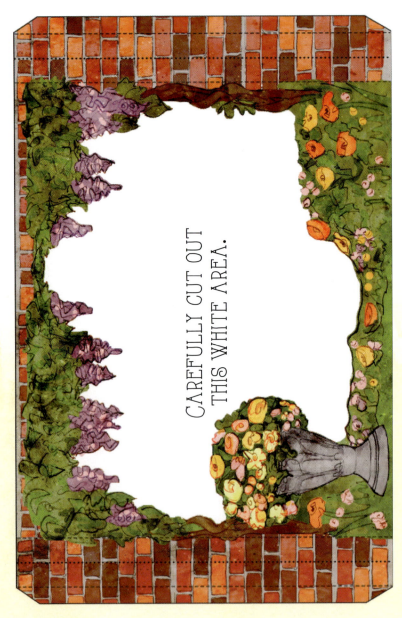

[PAPER GARDEN MODEL, CONCLUDED]

Section 4

"As long as you have a garden you have a future and as long as you have a future you are alive."
—FRANCES HODGSON BURNETT

Garden Games for Family and Friends

Mary, Colin, and Dickon spend hours each day outdoors in the garden. The secret garden is part of a larger parcel of property known as a park in British English. A park is a large area of land kept in its natural state. In the United States, a park is a large green area in a town designated for recreational use. Children in 19th century England would often head outdoors and enjoy their time by playing games. Here are a few that are sure to become favorites if you don't know them already.

Blind Man's Bluff

SUPPLIES

A blindfold

A favorite game in Victorian England, this game is a variation on "tag". Pick someone to be 'it' – this person wears a blindfold and tries to tag the other players. When you are 'it' and tag someone, try to guess who it is. Choose a smaller area to play in, and make sure there aren't obstructions or other hazards.

Red Rover

Number of players: 8 or more

Divide everyone into two teams. Have each team form a long line, holding hands, facing the other team. The teams should be about 20 or so feet apart. Each team takes turns "calling out" another player from the other team by saying "Red Rover, Red Rover, let <insert child's name> come over !" The called child leaves their team's line and runs as fast as they can toward the other line, trying to break through the held hands of the other team. If the child breaks through, they get to take someone back with them to their team. If they don't break through, they join the new team. When a team only has one person left, that person tries to break through the other team. If they do not, their team loses. If they do, they gain a new player and the game continues.

Character Study: Frances Hodgson Burnett

"I believe, of course, in magic."

—FRANCES HODGSON BURNETT

Frances Hodgson Burnett's life is a journey of transformation not unlike Mary's in The Secret Garden. Born in Cheetham, near Manchester, England, November 24th, 1849, Frances soon learned what it meant to make huge life transitions. When she was three years old, her father died and left her family penniless. Frances's mother did the best she could to keep her father's shop open, but it was futile – in 1865, at the age of 15, Frances emigrated to the United States with her mother and four siblings to live with her uncle in Knoxville, Tennessee.

The Hodgson family was under the impression that their brother and uncle had a thriving business in the United States, but when they arrived, they soon discovered that the "house" was nothing more than a log cabin, and the successful business was an illegal, shady one. The southern United States was ravaged by the Civil War; if it weren't for the kindness of good neighbors bringing them food and helping them survive in the postwar South, the Hodgsons would not have made it.

Frances began writing stories to help earn money for the family. By the time she was 19 years old, Frances was widely published in magazines and making a decent living.

In 1870 her mother died, and in 1972 she married Swan Burnett, a doctor. After their marriage they lived two years in Paris, where Frances had two boys. At one point, Frances and her family returned to the U.S. to live in Washington, D.C. It was there that she began to write novels, and later serialized them in a magazine known as St. Nicholas. They were extremely popular and were eventually published as books. She wrote over 50 books in all.

After raising her sons, she divorced her husband, returned to England, and purchased a big house with a huge garden, not unlike Misselthwaite. It was in this walled garden that Frances Hodgson Burnett wrote The Secret Garden. Within its pages she placed many of her own beliefs such as the power of positive thinking to change outcomes, the idea of magic, that good food and fresh air could rid one of almost any ill, and the notion of communication with animals.

As Frances wrote The Secret Garden, she was visited everyday by a red-breasted robin who would happily perch himself on a chair or on top of the table. She felt a deep connection to this particular bird and wrote him as a character into the pages of her tale.

Shortly before her death on October 29th, 1924, and just after The Secret Garden was published, Frances wrote a little book – called simply, *My Robin* – about the real robin from her walled garden at Maytham Hall in Kent, England.

Frances Hodgson Burnett ended up returning to the United States, where she lived on Long Island until her death of colon cancer in 1924.

She is greatly remembered for her well-known stories such as The Secret Garden, The Little Princess, and Little Lord Fauntleroy, as well as writing theatrical interpretations of these.

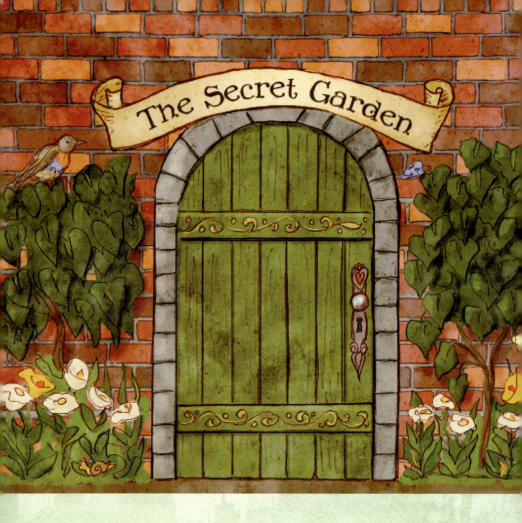

Come back to the Secret Garden again for more adventures and fun!

RESOURCES

We have provided a website for you to download patterns, paper cutouts, and other resources that you may need while enjoying this book.

Go to this http://www.audreypress.com/ebooks/secretgarden/

Once you register, you will arrive at the Secret Garden.

Click on the paper cutout or pattern you need to download, print, and use!

The following resources are available:

- Secret Garden Character Cutouts
- Seed Packets
- Felt Creature Patterns: Fox, Lamb, & Rabbit
- Wheelbarrow
- Paper Garden Model

(See examples of available printouts on the pages that follow...)

Secret Garden Character Cutouts

Seed Packets

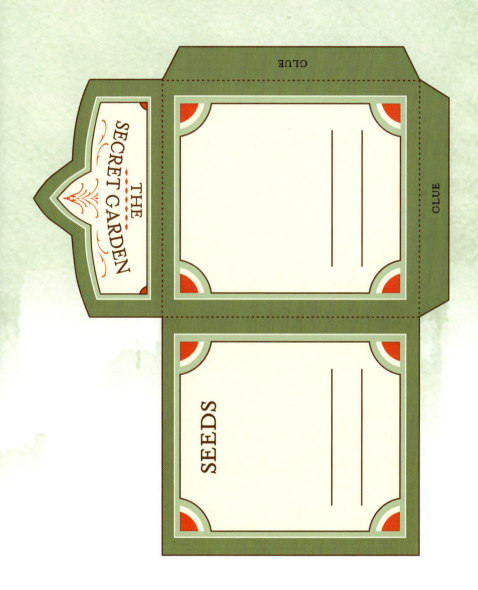

Felt Creature Patterns: Fox, Lamb, & Rabbit

Wheelbarrow

PAPER GARDEN MODEL

[MORE PAPER GARDEN MODEL]

Meet the Author

Valarie Budayr

Valarie Budayr loves reading and bringing books alive. Her popular website, <www.jumpintoabook.com>, inspires children and adults alike to experience their books through play, discovery, and adventure.

She is founder of Audrey Press, an independent publishing house as well as an Amazon and iTunes best-selling author. She has written *The Fox Diaries: The Year the Foxes Came to our Garden* and *The Ultimate Guide to Charlie and the Chocolate Factory*. Valarie is passionate about making kid's books come alive and encouraging families and schools to pull books off the shelves and stories off the pages.

Other Books and Adventures by Valarie Budayr

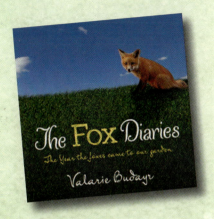

The Fox Diaries:
The Year the Foxes Came to Our Garden

Jump Into a Book presents:
The Ultimate Guide to Charlie and the Chocolate Factory

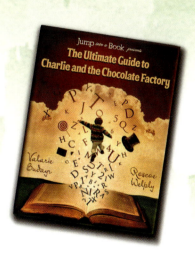

Available at Audreypress.com

Meet the Illustrator & Toymaker

Marilyn Scott-Waters

Marilyn Scott-Waters loves making things out of paper. Her popular website, www.thetoymaker.com, receives 2,000 to 7,000 visitors each day, who have downloaded more than six million of her easy-to-make paper toys. Her goal is to help parents and children spend time together making things.

She is the creator of a paper toy craft book series *The Toymaker's Christmas: Paper Toys You Can Make Yourself* (Sterling), and *The Toymaker's Workshop: Paper Toys You Can Make Yourself* (Sterling). She is also the co-creator with J. H. Everett of the middle grade nonfiction series, *Haunted Histories*, (Christy Ottaviano Books / Henry Holt Books for Young Readers). Ms. Scott-Waters illustrated *The Search For Vile Things* (Scholastic), and created paper engineering for *Pop & Sniff Fruit* (Piggy Toes Press).

Other Books and Adventures by Marilyn Scott-Waters

The Toymaker's Christmas:
Paper Toys You Can Make Yourself

The Toymaker's Workshop:
Paper Toys You Can Make Yourself

Haunted Histories

The Search for Vile Things

paper engineering for
Pop & Sniff Fruit

More Information at THETOYMAKER.COM

Audrey Press Credits

Thank you to all the members of Audrey Press who have taken part in this project.

Kitten Adventure Boggs	Editor and Graphic Designer
Becky Flansburg	Project Manager and Head Elf
Hannah Rials	Intern, Food Stylist, and Crafter

The Audrey Press Administrative, Technology, and Support teams are provided by BizEase Support Solutions:

Terry Green, *President of Bizease Support Solutions*
tlg@bizeasesupport.com

Caley Walsh	Websites
Theresa Scholes	Shopping Carts and Internet Marketing
Lara Nieberding	Administrative Online Support
Patty Dost	Online Support

PO Box 6113, Maryville, TN, 37802
www.audreypress.com
info@audreypress.com

www.jumpintoabook.com